Say No To Vanilla

all the best!

Warmly,
Dwight

The Five Keys to Living Life at Full Throttle

By Dwight Edwards

(www.highoctaneforthemind.com)

Copyright © 2013 Dwight Edwards

All rights reserved.
No duplication without permission

Print ISBN: 978-1-7907-1272-4

Table of Contents

Introduction

"The tragedy of life is what dies in the hearts and souls of people while they live."

Albert Einstein

Vanilla. There's nothing wrong with it. Really. In fact throughout the world on any given day it is by far *the* most requested flavor of ice cream. Both its taste and smell are enjoyed by most everyone.

But what goes through your mind when you think of the word "vanilla"? My guess is that it is an image that is neither highly revolting nor wildly exciting. Most likely it's kind of right there in the middle…pleasant, safe, comfortable, predictable, never in danger of an extreme. Just like far too many people's lives.

Take George for example. He is a middle aged dentist whose practice has done well. Very well for that matter. George works hard, is a good father, perseveres in a struggling marriage, enjoys a very comfortable lifestyle, and plays tennis three or four times a week. His life is envied by many who are looking in from the outside. But the inside is a different story.

He told me a little while back, "I don't have any real reason for getting up in the morning. Apart from my children, I see no purpose to my existence. Most days I'm bored to tears with my practice, my marriage sucks on the whole; tennis is about the only place I feel some sense of excitement. I have more material things than most people would ever dream of owning. But I can't shake the feeling that I want something more, something deeper - a sense of adventure, of purpose, of excitement. But I don't know how to get it."

On the other hand, there is Thomas. His existence is far different than that of George. He is a forty year old mechanic, father of three children. Unlike George, there is no surplus in Thomas's life. He and his wife make just enough to pay the bills, feed and clothe the family; and very occasionally go out to a movie. But that's it. No savings, no college fund, and certainly no money for vacations. Thomas feels like his life is on a perpetual treadmill called "survival." One pay check to the next...one job to the next...one mortgage payment to the next. On and on it goes. Thomas also feels that same gnawing emptiness and lack of purpose that George does, but has no idea how things could change. In fact, most days he doesn't even have time to think about it. Ironically; though George's and Thomas's *existences* are radically different, their *lives* are actually very similar – bone dry in regards to purpose and adventure.

And finally, there is Sharon. She is an attractive, young homemaker who is about the nicest, sweetest Southern Belle you'll ever meet. But it's the sort of niceness that almost makes you tired to be around. You get the sense that she's working overtime to exude an apple pie image; yet you never feel like you're getting the real her. In a rare moment of disclosure she once told me that the only way she could get her mother's approval growing up was to always be cheery and bright. She wasn't even allowed to cry publicly at her father's funeral. As she continued through life she discovered that the best way to keep her mother (and people in general) happy with her was to never risk being truly honest about how she felt and to maintain an ongoing aura of niceness. Be vanilla and the world will be vanilla back to you.

George, Thomas, and Sharon are all examples of what I mean by vanilla living. They are nice, respectable, responsible individuals whose pleasant exteriors can mask but not alleviate the aching emptiness of their inner world. Their greatest problem in life is not an overbearing mother, a difficult marriage, an unfulfilling profession, lack of finances, or anything outside of themselves for that matter. Their greatest problem is within. Deep down inside they have raised the white flag of surrender. Dream surrender.

What I mean by this is that somewhere along the line they each quietly relinquished that inner yearning in all of us for radical, go for broke, risk the farm, dream chasing. Slowly but surely they surrendered their souls to the god of unruffled living. The word that monitors their lives more than any other is *safety*. Safety in relationships, safety in reputation, safety in work, safety in finances, safety in... In a word, they have become vanilla-ized; for nothing is "safer" than vanilla. But then, they're not the only ones by a long shot.

Movie critic George Grella, in commenting on the tremendous successes of the James Bond movies, wrote, *"He* (Bond) *lives the dreams of countless, drab individuals."* No doubt he is on to something. Scores of people find temporary relief from their vanilla existence by going to a theater or putting in a DVD; and vicariously enjoying the adventure, action, and drama of a staged hero.

When I was growing up, my favorite show to watch after school was "Superman." For half an hour I could lose myself in the world of Kryptonite, leaping over tall buildings in a single bound, and the heroics of keeping the world safe from evil. Problem was, when the show was over so was the surrogate excitement!

Whether through video games, reality TV shows, action movies, etc.; our culture is increasingly satisfied to experience adventure secondhand. Though often unwittingly, far too many are seeking to slake their innate thirst for excitement at the fountain of others' risk taking. Yet the zestfulness of another can never fully satisfy or deeply thrill our own heart's yearning for tasting life's best. That can only be found by venturing out personally onto the playing field of personal dream seizing and actually stepping up to the plate. There the dangers are real and often great. But that is also the only arena where the highest rewards of real life are to be found. And may I add; there is infinitely better adventure and excitement to be had in real life than can ever be borrowed from a screen.

The fans cheering from the stands can enjoy the triumphs of their team on the field. But it is only those actually on the turf, playing the game, fighting the battle; who know first-hand the daring, the drama, and the exhilaration of personally competing for the win. The bench warmers share in the team's victory, but only the field warriors seize hold of the best their sport offers. Theodore Roosevelt put it as well as I have ever seen:

"It is not the critic who counts; not the man who points out how the strong man stumbled or where the doer of the deeds could have done them better. The credit belongs to the man who is actually in the arena; whose face is marred by dust and sweat and blood; who strives valiantly; who errs, and comes up short again and again, because there is no effort without error and shortcoming; who does actually try to do the deed; who knows

the great enthusiasm, the great devotion, and spends himself in a worthy cause; who, at the worst, if he fails, at least fails daring greatly. Far better it is to dare mighty things, to win glorious triumphs even though checkered by failure, than to rank with those poor spirits who neither enjoy nor suffer much because they live in the gray twilight that knows neither victory nor defeat."

Interestingly this same President Roosevelt understood well the lure and the dangers of vanilla living. In a letter from 1917 he writes, "*The things that will destroy America are prosperity at any price, peace at any price, safety first instead of duty first and love of soft living and the get-rich-quick theory of life.*" That, my friends, is a great description of vanilla living!

Vanilla living is a very, very seductive and enticing approach to life. But it is also deadly. Oh, it may not kill a person physically; but it reduces men and women to walking zombies, as we will see in the next chapter. It robs them of having a fire in their eye, a bounce in their step, an all consuming zeal for a great cause, and a reason to spring out of bed in the morning. It hypnotizes men and women under its alluring spell; and then sends them out to spend their few, short days on this earth in the studied avoidance of all significant risk-taking. And one has to question whether that is really living at all.

Someone put it well,

"There was a very cautious man
Who never laughed or played;
He never risked, he never tried,
He never sang or prayed.
And when one day he passed away
His insurance was denied;
For since he never really lived,
They claimed he never died!"

I love that poem! There is only one remedy for overcoming vanilla living. It is to become an out and out "vanilla buster." As Roosevelt put it, to leave *"the gray twilight that knows neither victory nor defeat"* and to be *"actually in the arena"*, having one's face *"marred by dust and sweat and blood."* It means abandoning the security and safety of the bleachers to enter into the dangers and glories of the playing field. It's about giving up small dreams and bite-sized ambitions so that we can take hold of dreams and ambitions big enough to make our stay on planet earth worthwhile. It's refusing to allow someone else to do our risk-taking and daring to live life at full throttle. It's about saying "no" to vanilla, and shouting "yes" to life.

Einstein was exactly right, *"The tragedy of life is what dies in the hearts and souls of people while they live."* The greatest tragedy for any of us is not death. That is a certainty for all, whether it come sooner or later. What is not certain is whether we will truly live, rather than merely exist. What is truly tragic is to spend our short stay on this earth having departed on the inside while continuing to exhibit counterfeit signs of life on the outside. Will we tamely settle for vanilla and wither on the inside; or will we grab life by the throat and demand it yield up to us the best it has to offer?

Jim Collins, in his best selling book "Good to Great", wrote an outstanding analysis of what separates the very best companies from the myriads of good ones. Out of over 1,400 companies that he and his team studied, they settled on eleven which ranked highest in their estimation. In this penetrating work Collins carefully details the central, key characteristics which marked each of these very best companies.

In a very similar way, this book is my humble attempt to do the same thing; only with people instead of companies. What are those few, non-negotiable traits which separate great existences from good or mediocre ones? What does it take to upgrade one's life from "good to great"? That is what this book is all about.

After almost five decades of reading numerous biographies, chatting with many remarkable individuals, and pondering the common threads of uncommon lives; I come up with five. They are not the only five important components to a great life; but they seem to be the five that are most foundational. So come my friend, let us begin the journey...

Say "No" To Vanilla

Chapter I

Vanilla Living

"The greater danger for most of us lies not in setting our aim too high and falling short; but in setting our aim too low, and achieving our mark."
Michelangelo

Tetrodotoxin. My guess is you've never heard of it unless you're in the medical profession. But the stuff will knock you out. Literally. It's the drug of choice in Haiti for turning people into zombies. For real...

Tetrodotoxin is a poison found in the puffer fish that is 160,000 times more potent than cocaine and 1,000 times more lethal than cyanide. But in very trace amounts it can be made into a powder which is capable of taking a person into such a deep sleep that it appears they have died. And this is how a zombie is created.

The process normally begins when someone contracts with the local mambo (voodoo witchdoctor) to target an enemy of theirs. This mambo then applies a white powder - which is a mixture of tetrodotoxin and other substances - in a place that the person will unknowingly come into physical contact with it. Often it is the doorstep of the house or the door handle. The white powder is unconsciously ingested into the person's body and soon causes them to go into a deep, deep sleep. So deep that it is easy to mistake them for being dead.

As is the custom in Haiti, these seemingly dead individuals are quickly buried above ground. But they are then secretly removed from their coffin after the funeral is over. Once revived, they are given another hallucinogen which essentially renders them will-less and under the control of their captor. They can be kept in this kind of trance-like state for decades, usually working on farms, unknowingly carrying out the commands given them. Only when the mixture of Tetrotodxin with other hallucinogenic drugs is withdrawn does the individual fully revive. There is at least one account of a person returning to his village decades after he had been laid to rest. Needless to say, this created no small stir among the villagers. All of this is documented by a Harvard ethnobiologist named Wade Davis in his books "Passage of Darkness: The Ethnobiology of the Haitian Zombie" and "The Serpent and the Rainbow".

But one doesn't have to go to Haiti to see a zombie. Fact is; they are all around us. Here are just a few examples:

Men and women who go through life living under the spell of continuously seeking others' approval.

Business persons who are sleepwalking – going through all the right motions, earning a respectable living; but utterly asleep to what would make them most alive as a person.

Wives and mothers who have died on the inside to their most cherished dreams, while on the outside continuing to dutifully carry out their allotted responsibilities.

Students who spend their days under the hypnotic influence of their peer group, afraid to ever break ranks and be who they really are deep within.

And perhaps most of all, the multitudes of men and women who are living their lives on "auto-pilot"; dutifully going through the same motions, faithfully carrying out the same responsibilities, unflinchingly following the same routine. But seldom, if ever, interrupting their utterly predictable existence with a new thought, a new risk, or a new adventure.

Indeed it is almost easier to spot who is *not* a zombie, than who is. Show me one man or woman with a fire in their eyes, a spring in their step, the ring of excitement in their voice, and a cause that launches them out of bed in the morning; and I will show you a hundred respectably disguised zombies, going through the motions of living while tragically disconnected from the passion and vitality that truly makes one alive. Prolific author John Gardner is exactly right when he writes, *"We have to face the fact that most men and women out there in the world of work are more stale than they know, more bored than they would care to admit..."*.

William Wallace led his fellow Scotsmen towards the overthrow England's control of Scotland in the late 1200's. In the movie depicting his story, aptly entitled "Braveheart", Wallace makes a tremendous observation the night before he is to be executed - *"Every man dies, not every man really lives."* There is a monumental differe-nce between living and existing, though far too few ever learn this distinction first hand.

How then does one taste the difference? How does one ensure that his or her few days upon this earth are not squandered on a zombie-like existe-nce of merely fulfilling rote responsibilities; but rather are spent in a white-hot pursuit of radical, go for broke, uniquely significant living? The starting point is learning how to recognize and resist the Tetrodotoxin of our souls. It's called "vanilla

4

living" – that subtle, yet oh so dangerous white powder of safe but inconsequential living.

So what exactly is "vanilla living"? Most often it is a minimal risk, maximum comfort, self-protective approach to life that craves security, safety, and immediate satisfaction above all else. As we saw earlier, Roosevelt well described it as, *"prosperity at any price, peace at any price, safety first instead of duty first and love of soft living and the get-rich-quick theory of life."*

On the other hand it can be a day to day, just getting by, colorless existence of resigned dreams and dashed hopes. In either case it is basically an approach to life whose loftiest goal is the enjoyment of earth, whose greatest value is personal and family security, and whose highest hope is surviving as comfortably as possible.

In large measure it is what French philosopher and mathematician Pascal called *"licking the earth."* What he meant by this is that it is man's futile attempt to satisfy the raging thirst in his soul through the fleeting pleasures and treasures of this earth. Ultimately, as Pascal demonstrates, it is a lick which brings a taste that can neither last nor fully satisfy. But let's face it. It is also a very, very tempting lick.

The undeniable reality is that there is a part in all of us that *loves* vanilla living. Certainly I find it in myself and cannot help but believe it is also in you, as well as every person. When I have to make the choice between sleeping awhile longer or getting up to bust it in an early morning workout, the vanilla part of me begs for sleep. And over time, it never stops begging regardless of how many times I drag myself to the workout.

When there is a difficult situation at work that requires confronting another, my vanilla side pleads to just let things go and keep peace at any price. And again, this vanilla propensity is never fully extinguished no matter how many times I risk confrontation.

In choosing a financial direction which requires risk for potential gain; a part in me always whimpers, "Don't risk any of what you've got, hold on to the sure thing at all costs." This whimpering, pleading, vanilla-loving part in all of us never grows up over time. Though at times we experience the joy and satisfaction of saying "no" to vanilla through well directed risk-taking; these victories never completely silence the cry of vanilla in the soul. But they can serve as powerful encouragements for future risk-taking. As William James put it, *"It is only by risking our persons from one hour to another that we live at all. And often enough our faith beforehand in an uncertified result is the only thing that makes the result come true."*

What then is the cure for a vanilla infected life? I believe it is to first understand why vanilla living is so enticing. Then secondly to understand why it is so dangerous. And finally, to know how to break free from its sweet, seductive stranglehold and become a "vanilla buster." In this chapter we will look at the first two issues.

Its Enticements – It seems to me that there are three primary allurements which seek to seduce all of us onto the vanilla path. They are ease, risk avoidance, and immediate gratification.

Easy Street

One of the most powerful enticements to vanilla living is that it is just flat easier. It's easier to not sweat than to sweat, to eat that piece of cake than pass it by, to spend rather than to save. And it's far, far easier to hold on to the familiar and comfortable than to exchange it for the unknown and unsure. As Elbert Hubbard put it, *"The reason men oppose progress is not that they hate progress, but that they love inertia."*

This is why one of the central components of vanilla living is "inertia." No movement, no hassle, no inconvenience, no risk,…and no real life - just existence. It is what transforms men from competitors to couch potatoes, women from avid readers to catalogue gazers, and kids from outdoor adventurers into video addicts.

All of us have a propensity towards laziness. In truth there is a wonderful deliciousness to it. To check out from personal responsibility, to put life on hold, to soak in the warm waters of lethargy; is a feast we all enjoy at some level. Tolstoy described it well during one juncture of his life, *"You can't imagine what a pleasure this complete laziness is to me: not a thought in my brain- you might send a ball rolling through it!"* But the temporary deliciousness of laziness always leaves the soul unfulfilled and often guilty. There is something about sweat and hard work and overcoming adversity that produces a depth of satisfaction in the human spirit which easy street living never can. This is why, when we look back on our lives, the times we most mentally savor are very often those junctures where life was hardest and we persevered. Malcolm Muggeridge observes, *"Contrary to what might be expected, I look back on experiences that at the time seemed especially desolating and painful with particular satisfaction. Indeed, I can say with complete truthfulness that everything I have learned in my 75 years in this world, everything that has truly enhanced and enlightened my experience, has been through affliction and not through happiness."*

Certainly there are needed times of rest and relaxation for all of us. Without them we will become burned out and ineffectual. But when unnecessary rest becomes our drug of choice for escaping the responsibilities, challenges, and opportunities of life; we have become vanilla-ized. And our lives become but a shell of what they could be. As Pascal put it, *"Our nature consists in motion, complete rest is death."*

Risk? – No Thanks

The second great seduction of vanilla living is the alleviation of risk-taking. Certainly there is a measure of excitement and adventure that risk-taking provides. But there is also a reluctance, if not dread, that many of us have towards entering the danger zone. Risk always involves danger of some kind. In risking confrontation with a loved one there is the danger of lost or withdrawn relationship. In risking a job change there is the danger of lost security and benefits. By saying what we feel most deeply, we risk the danger of being dismissed or scoffed at. On and on it goes. To actually go out and compete on the field brings the possibility of bruises, blood, and broken bones. Surely the bench is a better place to view the game. Indeed it is, if vanilla is the best one is looking for. But is that really enough in life for any of us?

While the bench provides an escape from the dangers of competition, it can never provide an escape from the cry of the heart. No amount of risk deferral can quiet the call of the wild echoing within every human being. Oswald Chambers was exactly right, *"Human nature, if it is healthy, demands excitement..."* Every human spirit is embedded with a yearning for unbridled, go for broke, push the edge living. This is part and parcel of our nature, and there is simply no way to eradicate its passionate presence within. But we can ignore it. And too often do.

Not long ago a survey was done among a large group of elderly men and women. The question was asked, "What three things would you do differently if you could live your life over?" They were then given a dozen or so possible answers to choose from. Guess what response ranked number one? *"I would have risked more"* was the runaway first place answer. How interesting! In the twilight years of life their greatest regret was not that they hadn't made enough money, hadn't visited enough countries, hadn't made a bigger name for themselves, etc. It was simply that they had played safe too often, had settled for vanilla too frequently, and too easily had chosen the safety of the bench rather than the dangers and glories of the field. But they couldn't escape their innate hunger for excitement even at eighty and beyond.

Risking always costs; but not risking costs even more in the long run. Paulo Coelho, the popular Brazilian novelist writes, *"Pitiful is the person who is afraid of taking risks. Perhaps this person will never be disappointed or disillusioned; perhaps she won't suffer the way people do when they have a dream to follow. But when the person looks back-she will hear her heart."*

I want it now

The third great seduction of vanilla living is immediate gratification. We love to know that whatever effort we expend on something will yield an immediate return. Human nature thrives on the assurance of predictability. Money placed in a savings account *immediately* begins drawing interest. A bite of something delectable *immediately* is savored by our taste buds. A click of the button and *immediately* the channel changes. We are far less excited about having to wait for a return. What would happen to alcohol sales if a drink didn't begin to affect a person's system until two days after they drank it?

We are the most "instant" generation in the history of the world. Instant coffee, instant breakfast, instant financing, instant messaging...no people since the beginning of time have had quicker access to what they want than us. Not that this is necessarily a bad thing. But the danger arises when immediate gratification is seen as normative and necessary for living life to the full. American writer Bill Bryson notes, *"To an American the whole purpose of living, the one constant confirmation of continued existence, is to cram as much sensual pleasure as possible into one's mouth more or less continually. Gratification, instant and lavish, is a birthright."* Ouch. But I believe he is right. On the whole we are a nation who believes that instant gratification is more an inherent entitlement than an occasional to frequent blessing.

The grave problem with living for instant gratification is that the best life has to offer is seldom immediately available upon purchase. In other words, there is almost always a waiting period before the reward for well-directed toil begins to kick in. A change in exercise and diet seldom has the immediate results one would like. But it does pay off. Good writing requires multiple, multiple drafts before the best is finally settled on. Every great skier was once a poor skier who refused to give up.

Look at the history of the world and progress. It required hundreds of experiments before the Wright brothers flew for the first time. Edison tried over ten thousand experiments before he found the right filament for the light bulb. On and on it goes. Those who want to seize hold of the best life has to offer must be willing to work harder and wait longer than the myriads satisfied with the offer of vanilla. And they must be willing to aim higher.

Laurence Shames, writer for the New York Times, offers this intriguing perspective on success and aiming high.

"John Milton was a failure. In writing Paradise Lost, his aim was to "justify the ways of God to men." Inevitably, he fell short and wrote only a monumental poem. Beethoven, whose music was conceived to transcend fate, was a failure, as was Socrates, whose ambition was to make people happy by making them reasonable and just. The

surest, noblest way to fail is to set one's standards titanically high. The flip side of that proposition also seems true. The surest way to succeed is to keep one's striving low. Many people, by external standards, will be "successes." They will own homes, eat in better restaurants, dress well and, in some instances, perform socially useful work. Yet fewer people are putting themselves on the line, making as much of their minds and talents as they might. Frequently, success is what people settle for when they can't think of something noble enough to be worth failing at."

I believe he is on to something very, very significant here. While we all want to be "successful"; we need to be careful that our successes are not merely shallow, external monuments to our unwillingness to set our standards *"titanically high."* As Michelangelo put it, *"The greater danger for most of us lies not in setting our aim too high and falling short; but in setting our aim too low, and achieving our mark."*

While the allurements of ease, risk avoidance, and immediate gratification are unquestionably attractive to all of us; their seductive white powder slowly but surely casts the soul into a deep slumber. It insidiously reduces people to walking zombies; and robs them of the passion, vitality, and significance that their lives were meant to be marked by.

In the final analysis vanilla living draws its victims in through four tentacles. It is *quicker* – immediate gratification. It is *easier* – less effort. It is *safer* – minimal risk. Finally, it is *simpler* – far less confusing. But is it really worth it? Is this the best life has to offer her voyagers?

Its Dangers - There are at least four important reasons why vanilla living, enjoyable as it may appear, is so dangerous.

It numbs us to our deepest desires. This Tetrodotoxin of the soul numbs us to the innate longings of our heart for radical, risk-taking, go for broke living. Every person is an adventurer at heart, imbued with a spirit of daring, and a hunger for scaling the heights of exuberant living. This is a non-negotiable part of human nature, one of the central colors streaking our souls. It will never ever be fully erased or extinguished, though its cry may become barely audible. To illustrate this truth the Danish philosopher Søren Kierkegaard created a parable of a wild duck flying northwards in the spring with all his fellow ducks. The Reverend Andrew Stirling describes it for us:

As they got over Denmark, which was Kierkegaard's home, they decided to land and take a respite. They landed in a farmyard where there were domestic ducks that had become part of the farm experience. This wild duck decided to take it upon himself to eat with these domestic ducks, and filled himself with food. He loved the life on the farm. Every day somebody actually brought food for you! Can you imagine that? There was a warm barn to go into at night with hay for bedding and other animals for company. This is great, thought the duck.

So, he ate more and more and more, and when it came time for his flock to fly off, the duck said, "Oh, actually, I would like to stay here a little while longer. Why don't the rest of you continue with your migration?" He thought, I am going to sit here and eat and get fat. So, he did.

On their way back south in the fall, the other ducks flew overhead and quacked and made noises and invited their friend to come back. But he said, "No, I am happy here. I am well fed. I have water, a barn, friends, I don't need to go with you." But then, he thought about it and decided that maybe he should go. He started to take off, but he was so fat he could only make it as far as the top of the barn. Finally, his wings gave out, and he dropped back down again.

The next spring, the flock came back again. All his friends were in the air, and they all called out, "Come, come and join us."

This time, he tried to fly, and he couldn't even get above the door. He was so fat, so happy, so complacent, and so his friends went on to their adventure in the north. Year after year, they flew overhead and invited him to join them, but he didn't. He couldn't move any more. After a while, he didn't even hear them or recognize them, and then he died.

That, my friends, is a perfect description of the numbing effect vanilla living has on the soul. One grows fat in the barnyard, stops taking any significant risks, and eventually dies; having become deaf to the call for higher living. Someone, having read Kierkegaard's fable, penned these lines –

"My soul is like a barnyard duck
muddling in the barnyard muck,
fat and lazy with useless wings.

But sometimes, when the northwind sings
and the wild ducks fly overhead,
it remembers something lost and dead.
It cocks a wary and bewildered eye
and makes a feeble attempt to fly.

Unfortunately it's fairly content
with the state it's in,
but it's not the duck it might have been."

But is it really true that we all have an innate yearning for adventure packed living? Do me a favor. Close your eyes and try to go down as deep within your soul as you can. What do you hear whispering to you, calling out your name? Perhaps you hear something like, "Write that book... record that song...become a mentor to an underserved child...start your own business, etc." Or do you hear, "Play safe, keep everything as comfortable and predictable as possible."? Or as you continue listening is it more, "Spread your wings and soar as high as the winds of life will take you."? Be still and keep listening. What do you hear? I rest my case. You and I were made for soaring, not safety.

What can and does happen though is that this innate longing to soar is not eradicated but submerged beneath the surface of vanilla living. The call of the wild in our heart is muffled by the shout of this world for a safe, predictable, non-threatening existence. The whisper in our soul to do something extraordinary with our lives becomes almost inaudible because of the sights and sounds of the barnyard. Yet this whisper, this cry, never goes completely away, however faint it may seem. And we will never be satisfied until we allow it to take us by the hand, lead us into the land of noble risk taking, and invites us to possess all the territory we are capable of. Antoine de Saint-Exupery, author of "The Little Prince", put it well, *"It is in the compelling zest of high adventure and of victory, and in creative action, that man finds his supreme joys."*

It neuters our potential influence. Vanilla lovers never become world changers. A great example of this is found in George Bernard Shaw's play, "Saint Joan" - the story of Joan of Arc. In Scene II there is an interchange between Joan and King Charles as she urges him to summon the courage to fight for France. She promises him, *"...I will put courage into thee."* To this he responds, *"But I don't want courage put into me. I want to sleep in a comfortable bed, and not live in continual terror of being killed or wounded. Put courage into the others, and let them have their bellyful of fighting; but let me alone."*

A few sentences later he says, *" I don't want to be any of these fine things you all have your heads full of: I want to be just what I am. Why can't you mind your own business, and let me mind mine?"* To this she responds, *"Minding your own business is like minding your own body: it's the shortest way to make yourself sick. What is my business? Helping mother at home? What is thine? Petting lapdogs and sucking sugar-sticks? I call that muck. I tell thee it is God's business we are here to do: not our own"*...

I believe she's exactly right. God has given all of us something vitally unique to contribute to this world. There is a song only you can sing, a poem only you can write, a niche only you can fill, and an influence that you and you alone can exert. No one can step in and read your script for you, or serve as your understudy in life. Your short stay on this planet is meant to leave it a different place than when you came in. *You matter...*not only because of who you are, but especially because of what you have to offer this needy, broken world. I plead with you on behalf of this world's inhabitants - Don't rob us of what you uniquely have to offer. Give us your deepest best!

One of the gravest dangers to actualizing our full potential and completing our total assignment here on earth is not vanilla living but vanilla poisoning. This what Scottish philosopher Thomas Carlyle was getting at when he said, *"Adversity is sometimes hard on a man, but for one man who can stand prosperity there are a hundred that will stand adversity."* In other words the white powder of prosperity is far more likely to comatose the inhabitants of earth than the blows of adversity. Not that prosperity is wrong in itself. Nor is comfort. Nor is pleasure. Nor is safety. Each has its legitimate and potentially healthy place in a well lived life.

But these things can so easily form the Tetrotodoxin which deadens our sensitivities to the radical, influential living that our souls most deeply long for. Slowly, usually imperceptibly, their mixture is ingested into our being, numbing our highest senses, and then lulling us into a sleep walking state.

As one considers the truly great influencers of history – Gandhi, Lincoln, Edison, Einstein, Mother Teresa, etc. – how grateful we are that they each managed to say no to vanilla. They didn't have to, but each chose to; and how different the world is today because of their noble risk taking. Einstein, for instance, could have contented himself with teaching a little high school math, puttering around in his garden, playing cards with his friends, and finding a hobby or two to fill up whatever time he had left over. Can you imagine the tragic difference *that* would have meant to the world? Fortunately for all of us, he chose to be a vanilla buster.

But the question has to be asked, "How many more Gandhis, Lincolns, Edisons, etc. were there *supposed* to have been?" Thoreau put it well, *"Most men lead lives of quiet desperation and go to the grave with the song still in them."* How many lives of noble influence never saw the light of day because their potential was buried in a vanilla casket? How many songs were never sung because quiet desperation controlled the vocal cords? Vanilla living affects more than just us.

It robs us of life's actual best. One of the greatest tragedies of vanilla living is that it unwittingly sacrifices what is *actually* best for what is *seemingly* best. Or to put it another way, superlative gratification is forfeited in the rush for immediate gratification. The fiery aliveness of giving oneself unreservedly to a noble cause is forfeited for the more immediate enjoyment of prolonged television watching. The deep seated satisfaction of intellectually stimulating reading is by-passed for the easier and quicker route of video playing. The clean joy of helping the underprivileged is exchanged for the lesser but easier happiness of a quick trip to the mall.

Again, this is not to say that television watching, video playing, or mall shopping is wrong. It is simply to say that we too often play the fool by going after this world's costume jewelry when the highest quality gold and silver is readily available. But the best requires more of us and usually takes longer to secure.

In my last book, "A Tale of Three Ships", I wrote about the crucial issue of an *unrecognized downgrade*. If you were flying business class and the flight attendant invited you to move up to first class, what would be your response? Probably very positive. But suppose you were flying first class and you were invited to move down to business class? None of us get excited over that scenario.

One of the great, great dangers of vanilla living is that it seduces its victims into believing that they are flying first class when they actually have been relegated to second or third class. They just don't recognize it. They have unwittingly downgraded from a daring, magnificent life to a safe, unruffled, existence. They have chosen safety over soaring. And that choice is plundering them daily of the best life has to offer.

It diminishes our legacy. Let me ask you a question. What do you most want said about you at your funeral? Ever really think about it? Or to put it another way, what single sentence do you want to best describe your short stay on this planet? This is no small issue. Does anyone really want their life to be summarized as, "He/she lived a risk free, relatively comfortable existence which will be completely forgotten within the next fifty years."? I think not. But that is the legacy of the vanilla flavored life. No risk, no danger, no setbacks, no bruises....and no remembrance.

Vanilla living leads to what I like to call a cotton candy life. It is a short sweet taste which has absolutely nothing to show for it at the end. And a cotton candy life makes a cotton candy difference in this world and leaves a cotton candy legacy in its wake. One of the saddest lines I know of is found in Somerset Maugham's book "Of Human Bondage." In it he refers to some elderly people whose lives had been spent on essentially a vanilla existence. He comments, *"These old folk had done nothing and when they died it would be as if they had never lived."* How tragic...how unnecessary!

Having seen the enticements and dangers of vanilla living, where does one go to escape its sweet stranglehold? There is only one remedy. To become a radical, fire breathing, untamable "vanilla buster." Let's see what that looks like...

Chapter II

Dreamers of the Day

"All men dream: but not equally. Those who dream by night in the dusty recesses of their minds wake in the day to find that it was vanity: but the dreamers of the day are dangerous men, for they may act out their dreams with open eyes, to make it possible."

T.A. Lawrence (Lawrence of Arabia)

No matter how hard he tried, he just couldn't shake it. Deep down he knew, but knew, that creating a rocket was not only possible; but that it would absolutely revolutionize the heights men would be able to reach in the air. Perhaps even travel to the moon. And he made the mistake of suggesting that in an article published by *The Smithsonian* in 1919. His name was Dr. Robert Goddard, a physics professor at Clark University.

The New York Times happened upon the article and wrote an editorial blasting the professor. They noted that space travel would be impossible, because without the atmosphere to push against the rocket, it would not be able "*to move an inch.*" Concerning Dr. Goddard they noted that his theory was rebuffed by "*the knowledge ladled out daily in high schools.*" But this public humiliation was not enough to send the professor packing or to cause him to give up on his seemingly impossible dream.

For twenty years Goddard experimented unsuccessfully with creating a rocket. Finally his first successful rocket launch occurred at his Aunt Effie's farm on Jan.18, 1926. The rocket shot up 184 ft. at 60 mph and lasted for two and a half seconds. His dream had finally been realized. In coming years it would continue to be refined many times over. And eventually man did fly to the moon, thanks to Dr. Goddard's refusal to give up on a dream that possessed him from childhood. A dream which was ridiculed by virtually everyone else. A dream which was seen as utterly impractical and which cost him deeply. But a dream he couldn't shake free from, no matter how impossible or unrealistic it seemed. Needless to say, the world has never been the same because of this dreamer who refused to go quietly into the night.

Robert Goddard is an outstanding example of the first characteristic of a "vanilla buster" - *the*

willingness to dream an extraordinary dream*.* In his graduation speech from high school he made a statement that became prophetic of his life's journey, *"It is difficult to say what is impossible, for the dream of yesterday is the hope of today and the reality of tomorrow."* As this trailblazing scientist so powerfully demonstrated; it is only those who are willing to dream the seemingly impossible who can accomplish the patently extraordinary. A life governed by bite-sized dreams makes a bite-sized difference in this world. President Woodrow Wilson put it well, *"We grow great by dreams. All big men are dreamers. They see things in the soft haze of a spring day or in the red fire of a long winter's evening. Some of us let these great dreams die, but others nourish and protect them; nurse them through bad days till they bring them to the sunshine and light which comes always to those who sincerely hope that their dreams will come true."*

But what is the difference between mere wishful thinking, fantasizing, and the kind of dreaming I am speaking of? Or perhaps better; what is the difference between the dreams we hold and those dreams which hold us? Only the latter are worthy of our all out pursuit, for they alone are the ones which most unerringly reveal our unique contribution on this earth. They are our "extraordinary" dreams.

What then, do these dreams look like? What are their characteristics and how does one go about

25

discovering them? These are the questions we will explore in this chapter.

First of all, an "extraordinary dream" is not necessarily a monumental, earth-shattering undertaking. Very often it will be a quiet, behind the scenes influencing of others and society. My observation has been that most people's extraordinary dreams are lived out in the shadows, away from broad public notice. Yet while they may not gain widespread attention, they gain what many never taste – the exhilaration and profound satisfaction of doing what one was made to do. As one teacher recently wrote me, "Isn't it something, that after 28 years of teaching, I still *love* what I am doing!" She has found her extraordinary dream, though most will never know of it.

One may have several extraordinary dreams in their lifetime, while another has but one. Our dreams, like our fingerprints, will vary from one individual to another. The great issue is not finding a dream of grandiose proportions, but finding that dream (or dreams) which makes us most alive as a human being. That dream will call you by name, will hold you in its clutches, will very possibly scare you to death, but will also excite you to the core. And it is a dream which enables you to say at the end of the day, "I know, but know, that *this* is what I was made for."

As I read the biographies of "vanilla busters" throughout history and chat with those of the present; it seems to me in each case their "dream" contains three central elements – *vision, passion,* and *action*. Or to put it another way, it is a dream that profoundly influences the head, the heart, and the hand.

Vision **(the head)** – This dream boldly and specifically envisions the details of what could be. This is where the head (the mind) comes in. In one of the greatest "dream" speeches of all time, Martin Luther King was very specific in the things he envisioned.

"I have a dream that my four little children will one day live in a nation where they will not be judged by the color of their skin but by the content of their character.

I have a dream that one day on the red hills of Georgia, the sons of former slaves and the sons of former slave owners will be able to sit together at the table of brotherhood.

I have a dream that one day, down in Alabama, with its vicious racists, with its governor having his lips dripping with the words of "interposition" and "nullification" -- one day right there in Alabama little black boys and black girls will be able to join hands with little white boys and white girls as sisters and brothers."

The kind of dream which captivates a vanilla buster is not an ethereal, nebulous, vague sense of what could be. It is a vision that has teeth; one that has clear, identifiable specifics in mind. Not necessarily all the specifics, but enough to captivate the imagination with its possibilities.

Walt Disney died five years before the completion of his famed Disney World. Following its dedication, two Disney executives were talking with each other. "Too bad Uncle Walt wasn't here to see this." remarked one. To this the other replied, "Oh but he did see it, that's why it's here." Exactly, but exactly! Vanilla busters see the specifics of what others assume could never be.

Passion **(the heart)** – This dream possesses not only the head but also the heart. It is not only informed, but also enflamed. It is characterized by an image in the mind *and* a fire in the bones. It's a fairly reliable rule of thumb that if your dream does not ignite you internally, you probably have not yet found that dream you were made for. Best selling author W. Clement Stone writes, *"When you discover your mission, you will feel its demand. It will fill you with enthusiasm and a burning desire to get to work on it."*

This is not to say that there won't be times of discouragement, weariness, even disillusionment. But none of these will be able to fully extinguish that deep seated vigor and fiery aliveness which comes from finding one's highest destiny.

This passion arises from two separate but united fronts. The first is that of being on the cutting edge of a new endeavor. There is something innately exhilarating about going where no man has gone before, of blazing a brand new path, or risking reputation for the sake of a radically new venture. Certainly it will be frightening, but nonetheless exhilarating. As Mark Twain put it, *"To do something, say something, see something, before anybody else - these are things that confer a pleasure compared with which other pleasures are tame and commonplace, other cheap and trivial."*

It can also mean infusing an old endeavor with brand new possibilities. Being on the cutting edge does not necessarily mean blazing a new path. It can just as much come from helping take an old path in new directions.

Every person was meant to be on the cutting edge of something – something uniquely designed for him or her. As famed Austrian psychiatrist and Holocaust survivor Victor Frankl put it, *"Everyone has his own specific vocation or mission in life; everyone must carry out a concrete assignment that demands fulfillment. Therein he cannot be replaced, nor can his life be repeated, thus, everyone's task is unique as his specific opportunity."* And it is only in the fulfilling of this unique and personal calling that life upgrades to the point of true exhilaration.

The second front is not that of being on the cutting edge but rather being in the center. What I mean by this is that there is a unique passion which arises in the soul when a man or woman comes home to what they were made for. It's what many call being "centered" - that intangible but undeniable sense of finding and being found by what we were made for. Alexander Solzhenitsyn said at age fourteen, *"I knew that I was born to write."* It is rare for someone to find their highest calling that early in life, but there is no escaping it once found.

The taste of being on the cutting edge of a fresh advance which springs forth from the depths of one's individual design is a cuisine unrivaled by the shallow and insipid finger foods of mere comfort and security. Coming home to what we were made for provides the soul with a vibrant rest found nowhere else. It is the ultimate win/win situation. That which springs forth from within us to most powerfully influence the world on the outside, is the very same thing that will most deeply satisfy our being on the inside. This is what Pablo Picasso was getting at when he wrote, *"It is your work in life that is the ultimate seduction."* In other words, finding and fulfilling one's unique calling in life will bring a greater and deeper ecstasy than any allurement this world has to offer. In his case, the joy he found putting paint on a canvass outstripped the pleasures of all the wine, women, and song he could find. Why? Because he had found his life's work and nothing could rival that.

I like to call this "hearing the click of the shotgun." This comes from observing the dog of a friend of mine; a dog who must be a zillion years old. The poor thing is riddled with arthritis, and it is just flat painful to watch him inch his way to his food bowl and back. But when my friend goes to his gun cabinet, pulls down his shotgun, and the dog hears the click of the shotgun; something just amazing begins to transpire. His ears go up, his tail begins to wag, new light comes into his eyes, and he begins to move far more quickly. And guess what? My friend still takes him hunting, and while he is out running after the prey, you would never know that anything is wrong. But once he comes home, and the guns are put away, he returns to his pitiful self.

Why this transformation? Very simple. My friend's dog is a hunting dog. His design in nature is to hunt and run down prey. No one taught him that this is what he should do; it is simply his inbred instinct. Nothing makes him more alive or energizes him more fully than the thrill of the hunt. If he were a herding dog, the click of the shotgun would mean nothing to him.

May I ask you a question dear reader? Have you heard the click of the shotgun? For you? Have you found that which energizes and excites your inner being like nothing else? It's there; please don't give up until you find it.

For me personally, it is speaking and writing. While growing up, this wasn't anything I aspired to in any shape or form. But over the years I've come to discover an undeniable reality. Nothing quite lights my fire like working with words to try and communicate ideas in fresh, memorable, and compelling ways. Whether it is through writing or speaking; hard as they at times, there is an undeniable "high" I find in communicating that outstrips anything else I try to do. For me, this is my *"click of the shotgun."*

Saying "no" to vanilla is far less difficult when it is being exchanged for that flavor which thrills a man to the core of his being and excites a passion within him deeper and richer than any he has ever known before.

***Action* (the hand)** – The final characteristic of this dream is that it inevitably translates into action. The dreaming I am speaking of here is in no way an escape from personal responsibility or a substitute for bone-wearying labor. There is substantial sweat equity required for any worthwhile vision to become reality. This is where the hand comes in. The extraordinary dream is not merely wishful thinking or heightened emotion. It is resolute action at the cost of time, sweat, and energy.

This is what T.A. Lawrence (Lawrence of Arabia) had in mind when he distinguished between the two different kinds of dreamers. *"All men dream: but not equally. Those who dream by night in the dusty recesses of their minds wake in the day to find that it was vanity: but the dreamers of the day are dangerous men, for they may act out their dreams with open eyes, to make it possible. This I did...*" I love the way he puts it, "*dreamers of the day are dangerous men...*" The reason? "*...for they...act out their dreams with open eyes, to make it possible.*" Lawrence demonstrated this powerfully in his own life. Having worked in the Middle East prior to WWI, he had spent time interacting with many disparate Bedouin tribes. He caught a vision of what could happen if these tribes would quit warring against each other and unite to defeat the Turks who controlled their country. He never lost sight of that vision, but actualizing it came at a tremendous price to this Englishman. It was this price, this sweat and pain equity that he was alluding to by the phrase, "*This I did...*"

It is only in the acting out of the dream that vision and passion become practical. Vision and passion may reside within the interior of a man or woman, but only action keeps the dream from being stillborn. And as we will see later in this book, it is the only through the strong combination of diligence and perseverance that one's unshakable dream becomes an undeniable reality.

All three of these components are critical. If vision is absent then there will be no clear direction for the unfolding of the dream. And whatever effort is expended will be unfocused or scattered. If passion is missing then there will be little enthusiasm for the great undertaking. And before long it will fizzle out. If action is lacking, there will be no concrete accomplishment and it really will have been but pie in the sky. But those dreams which are directed by clear vision, fueled by heart-felt passion, and carried out through relentless diligence make all the difference. These are the dreams that cause this world to take notice and leave the most lasting imprints. And they are the dreams which echo mightily throughout the deepest recesses of our being - "*This* is why you were born!"

How then does one go about finding their unique calling and extraordinary dream? The answer to this question is not easy and it certainly isn't mechanical or formulaic. The way it comes varies from individual to individual and therefore defies any single, cookie-cutter, one-size fits all answer. But here are some guidelines which I believe can help you in finding your dream.

Pray. I am aware that not everyone will agree with this, which is fine. But for myself, I believe that anything of significance in our lives requires God. I cannot write about this aspect of our lives without relating it to what I believe to be the Center of our lives and the universe. My first two books ("Revolution Within" and "Releasing the Rivers Within") lay out my understanding of true spirituality versus tired and rigid religiosity. In them I seek to demonstrate that man is a created being with a delegated purpose in life. This delegated purpose is designed and orchestrated by

God. Therefore, it seems to me that the first step in finding one's extraordinary dream should be an upward, dependent one. I realize that upward movement takes different forms for different people – prayer, meditation, inward listening, etc. **Seek to discover your dream, not create it.** Discovering one's extraordinary dream is a pursuit which must be both diligent and relaxed. As you earnestly seek to unearth your unique dream and calling, know that most likely it will find you before you find it. What I mean by this is that this dream will have been quietly and patiently preparing the soil of your heart long before its vision is ever planted in your mind. And when the dream hits you, it will not feel so much like you have discovered a new frontier as that you have rediscovered a long lost friend. There will be an intangible but very real sense of, "Yes...this is where I belong. Finally... I've found what I was made for. Undoubtedly... this is where I feel most centered." That's not to say that there won't be an accompanying sense of trepidation, insecurity, maybe even terror at the prospect of what now lies ahead. But even these things cannot prevent the soul from recognizing and enjoying its homecoming.

Joan is a stay at home mom with three children under six. Most days survival is her primary goal and understandably so. But something had been stirring in her that just wouldn't leave her alone. It was the vision of seeing her and other mothers with young children coming together one night a month to discuss a mutually agreed upon book and share their struggles and joys of motherhood. This dream, in her words, "kept hunting her down."

Finally she gave in, asked some other mothers what they thought about meeting together, and the first group was quickly born. Soon other groups like theirs began springing up. And now dozens of young mothers are benefiting tremendously each month from the dream that Joan could not shake. And, as she told me the other day, "It just feels like this is what I was made for!" She had discovered her extraordinary dream rather than trying to create one.

It is absolutely imperative therefore, that one not frantically rush to discover this dream. Diligently pursue finding it - yes. But in the pursuit beware of the temptation to speed things up by subtly (and usually unconsciously) creating a dream of one's own making. Too many people have settled for a second tier dream of their own invention and thereby missed the first tier one they were made for. And second tier dreams can never bring first tier satisfaction.

A good way to begin finding one's first tier dream (i.e. extraordinary dream) is to ponder how you would answer the following questions:

1. What would you most like to do if money were not an issue?

2. What would you most like to do if family responsibilities were not an issue?
3. What would you most like to do if geographical location was not an issue?
4. What most easily energizes and excites you? What topic of conversation brings new light to your eyes?
5. What non-required topic(s) do you find yourself most often reading about?
6. What work, though still tiring, leaves you energized rather than drained?
7. What quietly nags at you from within during times of reflection upon your life?
8. If you had to get a graduate degree, what would you most *enjoy* studying?
9. What would the people who know you best say that you most enjoy doing? Are best at?
10. What are you most afraid to admit that you would most enjoy accomplishing?

The answer to these questions should help to narrow down the leading candidates for your extraordinary dream.

Take inventory of your gifts, talents, and desires. Whatever your extraordinary dream is, it will fit you and you will fit it. It will be something you are uniquely given the gifts and passion to accomplish. Should Michael Jordan have been an engineer? Probably not. Should Einstein have played basketball? Surely not. Should Michelangelo have been an accountant? You get my drift. These men could have tried hard to perform the roles I just mentioned, but it would never have fit them. Why? Very simply, it's not what they were gifted for.

Fulfilling one's extraordinary dream will undoubtedly require much hard work; but when this dream matches one's personal uniqueness and giftedness, its required work will energize a person more than drain them. And they find a joyous fulfillment in that labor which keeps them from wandering in search of something else. This is what Harvey MacKay was alluding to when he wrote, "*Find something you love to do and you'll never have to work a day in your life.*"

This is where one might seriously consider taking some of the tests out there for aptitudes, temperaments, vocations, etc. I took one the other day just for grins and was amazed how accurately it described me, my abilities, and what vocations I would be good at.

None of these tests are infallible, nor do they perfectly gauge any one person. But they can be very helpful in narrowing down the field of possibilities so one has a clearer focus on what to be considering.

Another important step in this is to ask individuals who know you well (parents, teachers, trusted friends, etc.) what things they notice you do especially well and what things appear to most fulfill you. Often times others can see our unique giftedness before we can.

Above all else, remember the words of Oscar Wilde – "*Be yourself; everyone else is already taken.*" You are created, gifted, and impassioned with the ability to do something uniquely well. To do something only *you* can do. Wilde is right, "*...everyone else is already taken.*" Don't try to play someone else's hand. Bring all *your* gifts, bring all *your* talents, bring all *your* personality, bring all *your* passion to the card table of life and lay them all out for all to see. And whether things work out the way you hope or not, a far more important issue will have been settled. You will have had the courage to be yourself, to play your part, to follow your star. And no one can do more than that!

Try to touch bottom as to what you would most like to do. What I mean by this is that it can be very, very difficult to get down to the depths in our being where our most vital dream lies. It is much like swimming and trying to touch bottom in very deep water. You're not sure how far down the bottom is, so you swim down to see if you can touch it. But often there's comes a point where you haven't hit bottom yet and you're afraid to go down any further, so you shoot back up to the top.

I really believe that this is true of far too many people in their pilgrimage through life. Comparatively few of us ever go down deep enough to look our most important dream in the eye, call it by name, and bring it back up to the surface. It requires tremendous courage to make it that far. Julia Cameron puts it so well, *"Each of us has an inner dream that we can unfold if we will just have the courage to admit what it is. And the faith to trust our own admission. The admitting is often very difficult."*

What things keep us from touching bottom in finding our dream? We have already mentioned courage, which is absolutely crucial. Another is the fear of it being impractical. This one is huge! I can't tell you how often I have seen people come right to the brink of discovering their extraordinary dream only to lose it in the sinkhole of practicality. After speaking at a school recently, a teacher sent me the following email from one of her students, a senior in high school –

"I realized I have been looking at my future completely wrong. ...I now know law is definitely not for me. I always thought I would love psychology and helping others who have went through difficult situations as I have but I was looking at the

practical before my actual dream and he really makes me believe I can achieve it."

For one to find their extraordinary dream, the issue of practicality must be temporarily set aside. This young girl had been so focused upon the financial benefits of being a lawyer that her extraordinary dream almost slipped by. More extraordinary dreams have been assassinated by the issue of practicality than any other single thing. Of course it seems impractical, of course it's hard to see how it could ever work out, of course others will scorn it as being unrealistic; otherwise it wouldn't be a dream big enough to be worth your while. There were hundreds of reasons why the rocket should never have been invented. Just none big enough to stop Dr. Goddard from fulfilling his extraordinary dream! As Walt Disney put it so well, *"If you can dream it, you can do it. Always remember that this whole thing was started with a dream and a mouse."*

Another huge detriment to finding one's dream is the fear of what others will think, especially loved ones. I have had many men tell me over the years, "If I told my wife what I really, really would like to be doing, she would flip out." Or students who have told me, "If I majored in what I would most like to do, my parents would cut off my tuition." People's receptivity to our extraordinary dream can be not only disheartening, but also deafening. It is very difficult to hear the quiet whisper of one's dream in the soul while inwardly churning over how others will respond to it. Fear of criticism can have a tremendously paralyzing effect on being able to reach out and take hold of what we were made for. Abraham Lincoln put it well, *"If I care to listen to every criticism, let alone act on them, then this shop may as well be closed for all other businesses."*

41

Finally there is the fear of being disappointed. What is the point of going down deep within, discovering one's extraordinary dream, bringing it back up to the surface, only to find that the circumstances of life seem to obliterate the possibility of ever fulfilling the dream? As one woman told me, "This is like window shopping. What's the point of going out to look at things you know that you can never have? What's the value in me finding my extraordinary dream when I know my life will never allow me to chase after it?" John Grisham spent years as a lawyer while writing on the side. It became increasingly clear to him that his real love was being an author. But initially he could never have supported himself and his family only by the sales of his books. It would have been easy for him to shut down his dream of writing and to have returned fully to the world of law so that he wouldn't have been disappointed that his dream of writing never came to pass. Obviously he made a great choice to say 'no' to vanilla!

At one level this is a very understandable fear. None of us wants to be disappointed. But is it really a better alternative to never know that which will most enflame our being, heighten our existence, and cause our deepest parts within to sing for joy? Is it really better for us to keep under wraps the means to a radically centered and purposeful life, just to avoid the possibility of disappointment? Does never knowing what we were most meant to do really bring us a better quality of life than knowing? Clearly not. It may bring us a quieter soul, but not a fuller one. And the reality is that almost everyone can chase their extraordinary dream to one degree or another. We may not be able to make it our full time job, but we can still pursue it on the side. We can push it along incrementally. And one never knows where that may lead to.

Be open to a dream that could totally disrupt your life. This is one of the most difficult parts of the whole equation. An extraordinary dream always comes at an extraordinary price. To resolutely take hold of what one is made for will very often turn our world upside down; and possibly that of others around us as well. And therein lies one of the greatest difficulties – the impact our dream might have on others' lives.

A friend told me the other day about a dream he has and then followed it up with, 'If only I didn't have a wife and kids I would go for it right now." That's very understandable and he is to be commended for his sense of responsibility. But I wonder if he won't become another in the long line of individuals who assume their dream will cost others so much that isn't worth the pursuit. And so the dream is put to bed in the dormitory of the soul, never to disturb anyone else. But never to excite, enflame, or energize the person with a reason for living that outstrips anything they have ever known before. Though they may seek to find a substitute life purpose, none can resonate as deeply or passionately as the one they have said "no" to.

Also, we can't know the potential good our dream might bring to others as well. As I told my friend, "But what a great gift you would be giving your children - a husband and father fully alive, more centered than ever, and daily demonstrating the courage and persistence of pursuing an extraordinary dream. Isn't this what you want your children to do? The most influential thing you can do then is model it." We'll see what happens but every indication is that he is in the process of taking hold of his dream.

There is a wide variety of disruptions one's dream may bring. It may be *vocational* disruption – leaving a secure, comfortable job for the unrealized promise of what could be. This is exactly what John Sculley did in 1983 when he left a very prestigious position at PepsiCo to become president of a young, upstart company called Apple Computers. What caused him to take the risk? It was a question Steve Jobs, co founder of Apple goaded him with. "Do you want to spend the rest of your life selling sugar water, or do you want to help change the world?" He took the dare to be a world changer and followed his extraordinary dream.

There is very often *relational* disruption as we have just alluded to. Parents and spouses are very often unenthused, to put it mildly, by this new vision and direction. There can be *geographical* disruption – pulling up stakes which are deeply and securely driven, to move to a brand new location to make friends with brand new people and to start brand new all over again. Not many people get excited about that. But our country was settled by risk takers such as that. Or *financial* disruption; learning to live on a substantially shrunken budget in order to pursue this extraordinary dream. Dream chasing is an immensely practical issue with immensely practical costs. If one doesn't think that's true, it may be because they've never tried it.

There is no shortage of reasons why one shouldn't pursue their extraordinary dream. There normally is no lack of people to tell us why the dream can't work. Much of the time people in power dismiss the dream as impractical or unnecessary. Consider some of the following historical examples:

"There is no reason anyone would want a computer in their home." Ken Olson, president, chairman and founder of Digital Equipment Corp., 1977

"This 'telephone' has too many shortcomings to be seriously considered as a means of communication. The device is inherently of no value to us." Western Union internal memo, 1876

"Who the hell wants to hear actors talk?" H.M. Warner, Warner Brothers, 1927

"Heavier-than-air flying machines are impossible." Lord Kelvin, president, Royal Society, 1895

"Drill for oil? You mean drill into the ground to try and find oil? You're crazy." Drillers who Edwin L. Drake tried to enlist to his project to drill for oil in 1859

Or my favorite – *"We don't like their sound, and guitar music is on the way out."* Decca Recording Co. rejecting "The Beatles", 1962

There will always be a standing-room-only crowd to tell us why we should stop chasing the wind and get on with real life in the real world. And all these hindrances can become very convincing. But none of them can completely still the internal restlessness of a dream being put on hold. None of them can offer a replacement for the joyous passion of daring to dream the extraordinary dream. And none of them can provide that whisper in our inner ear, echoing forth from profoundly satisfied parts deep within, *"This* is the part you were born to play."

It is only the dreamers of the day who know whereof I speak. They are life's first-stringers, captivated by a life-transforming vision of what could be, enflamed by possibilities temporarily out of grasp, and energized to attack their dream with unreserved diligence and relentless perseverance. Most of them will never become famous or wealthy. But they will taste what so many around them never do – the deep joy of genuinely centered living. These vanilla busters refuse to merely exist in the valley of safe, routine, colorless living; but rather to soar to the fresh, unexplored heights of actualizing their extraordinary dream. They and they alone understand what Thoreau was talking about when he wrote, *"Our truest life is when we are in dreams awake."*

The extraordinary dream infuses men and women with extraordinary vitality and an extraordinary purpose for living. But it also thrusts them in the position of desperately needing extraordinary wisdom. And it is to this that we turn next.

Say "No" To Vanilla

Chapter III

Coloring Outside the Lines

"If at first, the idea is not absurd, then there is no hope for it."

Albert Einstein

Hard as he tried, he couldn't seem to break out of the pack. He easily worked as diligently as any of his fellow competitors, but just couldn't get ahead. Unless something happened, he was destined to be just another outstanding French skier among several outstanding French skiers on an outstanding French Olympic ski team.

But Jean Claude Killy is a vanilla buster at heart and he determined that he would do everything he possibly could to get to the next level. And so he began to dare to color outside the lines, to take the risk to think in fresh and unconventional ways. He started experimenting with some radically different techniques to see if he could find a winning edge.

He discovered three things that helped him to increase his times. But they all flew directly in the face of conventional skiing. He found at times that shifting his weight uphill improved his turns. Secondly, he discovered that keeping his skis apart in certain situations helped his speed and balance. Finally, he began using his poles to accelerate his speed and not simply to make his turns. All of these changes were completely contrary to how he had been taught to ski and certainly would not win him favor with the French coaches. But they might win him races. And, in fact, they did. In 1968 he won three gold medals in the Winter Olympics; a record matched by only one other in Olympic ski history. In 1967 and 1968 he was the World Cup champion, and totally dominated the sport until his retirement in 1968.

Killy has gone on to be a very successful businessman. And his same willingness to think outside the box and to risk innovative change has served him well in the corporate world. In a recent interview he discussed the most important things he had learned for business success:

"Win some, lose some. The object is to win more than you lose, but never give up. Never, ever give up. Secondly, the answer is always there. The problem is to find it. Not to find it is an excuse for not succeeding. Every young kid who worked with

me, I told 'Find the answer'. Not to complain, just find the answer please. There is always an answer."

Jean Claude Killy is a great example of the second main characteristic of a vanilla buster – **the willingness to color outside the lines.** Or to put it more commonly, to think outside the box. Extraordinary dreams do not come to fruition through cautious, conventional thinking. They require the daringness to launch out in new directions, the audacity to believe in one's own original thinking, and the refusal to rest until the best possible way is found. Like Killy, vanilla busters are respectful of the old ways but not enslaved to them. And when they see a new possibility rising out of the sand, they do not retreat in fear but rush forward in hopeful anticipation.

What exactly does it mean to "think outside the box" and "color outside the lines"? While there are many different ways to describe it, I like to define it as this – *"The courage to re-examine old assumptions, the eagerness to explore new avenues of thought, and the perseverance to exhaust all possibilities."* Let's take a closer look.

The Courage to re-examine old assumptions

This is the way we've always done it

Few statements sabotage the possibility of new advances more than this one. To do it the way it has always been done, to stay within the confines of what has previously been established, to color within carefully safe-guarded lines; these all provide a security and comfort which is particularly addictive to the play-safe soul. After all, if you are careful to never stray outside the lines you will ward off the danger of being criticized for rash or dangerous thinking. Staying within the lines insures that a nice, predictable, well-ordered painting will emerge. But the truly great masterpieces belong only to those who dare to venture outside the lines and who are willing to risk ridicule and criticism for the high adventure of fully releasing their deepest colors. As Neil Simon put it, *"If no one ever took risks, Michelangelo would have painted the Sistine floor."*

Vanilla lovers relish the security of inside-the-lines living; while vanilla busters exult in the opportunity to mightily dispense their unique and noble passions, whether inside the lines or not. As I noted in the last chapter, it is the difference between a life dedicated to safety versus soaring.

As in all things there is an important balance here. Willingness to think outside the box does *not* mean disrespect for the box. There is no valor or benefit in dismissing something simply because it is part of an established tradition. The fact that it is inside the box may well mean it has stood the test of time successfully. G.K. Chesterton put it well, *"Don't ever take a fence down until you know the reason it was put up."* Killy didn't toss out all conventional skiing techniques. In fact; most of the time it was those "inside the box" skills which he utilized very successfully. But he wasn't afraid to step outside the norm when it was necessary for peak performance.

While it is critical to maintain respect for the box, it is equally important not to idolize it. Somerset Maugham put it well, *"Tradition is a guide and not a jailer."* This is so, so true. Tradition serves us well when it provides a compass but not chains. Yet far, far too many people live their lives shackled to beliefs and practices of the past that have outlived their usefulness. What causes a person to do this? Let me suggest three main reasons.

False Humility – "Who am I to think that I could know better than the experts before me?" Or, "If this is true someone else would have already discovered it." And still yet, "I'm not smart enough to be able to come up with something significantly better." All these sentences have the ring of humility in them but not the real substance. True humility is never thinking less of ourselves than is accurate; but boldly stepping up to the plate and fully acknowledging both the good and the bad in our lives. John Ruskin put it so well, *"I believe the first test of a truly great man is his humility. I do not mean by humility doubt of his own power or* *hesitation in speaking his opinion. But really great men have a feeling...that the greatness is not in them but through them...*"

Why is it so surprising to think you might actually stumble across something radically different and new? When was it decreed that something like that was out of your league? Are you afraid that kind of thinking is arrogant on your part? Here's what is truly arrogant – believing that you *know* what your intellectual limits are and refusing to believe that you could move past them. There is absolutely no reason that you cannot discover other possibilities not yet seen by others.

Fear of Making a Mistake – It is a frightening thing to leave the safe harbor of tradition and to launch out into the risky, wind blown waters of non-traditional thinking. Suppose one takes the risk to think outside the box only to have their conclusion(s) proved inadequate or patently wrong? Is it really worth the embarrassment, the ridicule, the wasted effort, and the renewed self-doubt that will accompany one's failed attempts to color outside the lines?

Far too many have decided that it is. I have noticed this especially to be true in academic circles. Far, far too many scholarly books, articles, journals are written frozen in fear of peer response. This means that one's writing is done with an invisible critic looking over the shoulder, and the goal shifts from communicating what is most

54

radically alive within to what is most palpably certain to retain peer acceptance.

Keeping one's reputation intact, avoiding the shame of exposed misjudgment, and the security of staying safely within the harbor of tradition are more than enough reasons to stay anchored at home. But the reality is that it takes tremendous courage to pull up stakes and venture forth into the highlands of fresh and original thinking. Swiss psychologist Paul Tournier put it well, "...*in all fields, even those of culture and art, other people's judgment exercises a paralyzing effect. Fear of criticism kills spontaneity; it prevents men from showing themselves and expressing themselves freely, as they are. Much courage is needed to paint a picture, to write a book, to erect a building designed along new architectural lines, or to formulate an independent opinion or an original idea.*"

But what are the alternatives? Does anyone really want it to be said about them at their funeral, "So and so never offended anyone with their originality. They carefully stayed within the confines of the accepted norms of the day. You could always count on them to be safe, unthreatening, and devoid of anything innovative"? Yet this is the legacy that those who live in fear of making a mistake are on the verge of leaving.

Laziness – Again, I know it is harsh when put this way but I believe it is an undeniable reality.

One man has defined tradition as *that which enables men to act without thinking.*" While I think this is probably an overstatement of the case, he does make a vital point. If one wants to live life with all their thinking pre-arranged, their risk taking reduced to the bare minimum, their intellectual sweating eliminated; then enslavement to tradition will pretty well do the job. But to live life as it was designed to be lived, to "max out" in all that our humanity affords; requires that the great gift of the human mind be mightily exploited. It is undeniably hard work to think well, but our days on this earth can never be fully maximized without it. This is exactly what Henry Ford was referring to when he said, *"Thinking is the hardest work there is, which is probably the reason so few engage in it."*

It takes tremendous mental effort to color outside the lines. Or at least it should. First there is the intellectual rigor of deciding whether it is even necessary to think outside the box in a given situation. There is no valor in thinking outside the box just for the sake of appearing progressive or radical. Many times the best course of action is to remain within the box; which sometimes requires far more courage than venturing out.

Then there is the mental fatigue that comes from attempting to exhaust all possibilities. On top of all this is the internal tiredness that all true creative thinking brings. But it is a unique kind of tiredness – it both energizes and drains at the same time. Few things are more invigorating than the fresh discovery of a new paradigm or plan of action. Yet this invigoration rarely comes without a high price tag. Almost inevitably it involves hard, rigorous, imaginative analyzing and reflecting that saps one's interior strength. But it is so, so worth it. Personally, nothing exhausts me more than the mental taxation writing requires. Yet nothing invigorates and energizes my inner being like finding a fresh and creative way to express a thought.

In summary, we have seen that it requires tremendous courage to re-examine old assumptions and to refuse to allow unexamined tradition to have the final say in what we think and do. As G.K. Chesterton put it so well, *"Tradition means giving votes to the most obscure of all classes, our ancestors. It is the democracy of the dead."*

The eagerness to explore new avenues of thought

Thinking outside the box not only requires the courage to re-examine old assumptions; it also must include the eagerness to explore new avenues of thought. I use the word "eager" very purposefully. It is one thing to be *open* to exploring new avenues of thought; it is a very different thing to be *eager* to do so. Vanilla busters throughout history have been far more than passive observers, politely amenable to the possibility of a new way of viewing things. They have been (and are) passionate seekers of the new and better way, undaunted travelers along the pathway of truth, unafraid to venture down the most obscure trails of innovation if they hold potential. Their credo is well summarized by one of the greatest outside the box thinkers of all time, Thomas Edison - *"If there is a way to do it better, find it."*

This principle is well illustrated in the life of Norman Cousins as described by "Today in the Word",

In The Anatomy of an Illness: As Perceived by the Patient, Norman Cousins tells of being hospitalized with a rare, crippling disease. When he was diagnosed as incurable, Cousins checked out of the hospital. Aware of the harmful effects that negative emotions can have on the body, Cousins reasoned the reverse was true. So he borrowed a movie projector and prescribed his own treatment, consisting of Marx Brothers films and old "Candid Camera" reruns. It didn't take long for him to discover that 10 minutes of laughter provided two hours of pain free sleep. Amazingly, his debilitating disease was eventually reversed. After the account of his victory appeared in the New England Journal of Medicine, Cousins received more than 3000 letters from appreciative physicians throughout the world.

Or take, for example, the story of a secretary who revolutionized her profession by her passion to find a better way to do things -

Bette Nesmith had a good secretarial job in a Dallas bank when she ran across a problem that interested her. Wasn't there a better way to correct the errors she made on her electric typewriter? Bette had some art experience and she knew that artists who worked in oils just painted over their errors. Maybe that would work for her too. So she concocted a fluid to paint over her typing errors. Before long, all the secretaries in her building were using what she then called "MistakeOut." She attempted to sell the product idea to marketing agencies and various companies (including IBM), but they turned her down. However, secretaries continued to like her product, so Bette Nesmith's kitchen became her first manufacturing facility and she started selling it on her own. When Bette Nesmith sold the enterprise, the tiny white bottles were earning $3.5 million annually on sales of $38 million. The buyer was Gillette Company and the sale price was $47.5 million. (Crossroads)

This kind of eagerness to explore new avenues of thought requires at least two central predispositions which are crucial for success:

A willingness to embrace the absurd - The ability to color outside the lines begins with a commitment to not short sheet any idea, regardless of how big a stretch it might seem to be. This doesn't mean that the idea won't be dismissed at some point, but not before it's had its full say. And to do this is no small accomplishment. There are two reasons for this.

First of all, there is in most of us a natural inclination to be at least somewhat cynical toward radically new ideas. John Locke was exactly right when he wrote, *"New opinions are always suspected and usually opposed, without any other reason but because they are not already common."* The vast majority of us are "initial skeptics"; at least somewhat distrustful of novel thoughts or approaches. Yet it is interesting to note how quickly outside the lines thinking can become the accepted norm once the risk is taken. Take for instance the following examples:

"I have traveled the length and breadth of this country and talked with the best people, and I can assure you that data processing is a fad that won't last out the year." The editor in charge of business books for Prentice Hall, 1957

"The concept is interesting and well-formed, but in order to earn better than a 'C', the idea must be feasible." A Yale University professor in response to Fred Smith's paper proposing reliable overnight delivery service. (Smith went on to found Federal Express Corp.)

"So we went to Atari and said, 'Hey, we've got this amazing thing, even built with some of your parts, and what do you think about funding us? Or we'll give it to you. We just want to do it. Pay our salary, we'll work for you.' And they said, 'No'. So then we went to Hewlett-Packard, and they said, 'Hey, we don't need you. You haven't got through college yet.'" Apple Computer Inc. founder Steve Jobs on attempts to get Atari and H-P interested in his and Steve Wozniak's personal computer.

"The wireless music box has no imaginable commercial value. Who would pay for a message sent to nobody in particular?" Davis Sarnoff's associates in response to his urgings for investment in the radio in the 1920's.

The propensity of so many is to play safe, to not rock the boat, and to color safely within the lines. Vanilla busters however thrive on seeing things in new and fresh ways, imagining what could be, and taking the risk to color outside the lines. And the kind of coloring outside the lines that usually proves most fruitful very often begins by appearing most absurd. Absurd, because it flies in the face of what is presently believed. Absurd, because nobody else has ever proposed something like this. Absurd, because there are a million reasons why it could never work. Absurd, absurd, absurd... When Robert Fulton tried to explain his innovative vision of a steamboat to Napoleon, the

French general's response was, *"What, sir, you would make a ship sail against the wind and currents by lighting a bonfire under her decks? I pray you excuse me. I have no time to listen to such nonsense."*

Yet this seeming absurdity may in fact be one of the clearest evidences that we are on to something genuinely significant. The kinds of dreams and thoughts that have the greatest impact are very often ones that are farthest removed from the tired, normative, outworn way of approaching things. This is exactly what Einstein was referring to when he wrote, *"If at first, the idea is not absurd, then there is no hope for it."* His simple point being that ideas big enough to make a marked difference are usually perceived in the beginning as being so outrageously big that they are easily discounted as being "absurd."

Therefore, if your extraordinary dream or new idea seems initially ridiculous, it may be one of the best possible signs that you are on the right track. Instead of shrugging it off as too far out there; rush upon it with all your might, squeeze it as hard as you can until it yields up to you its full promise. In doing so you may well find that it provides you with the deep seated satisfaction of a fulfilled dream. Or you may discover that it was indeed a phantom; in which case you will be disappointed, perhaps greatly. But hear me well. *At least you tried!* And the contentment of knowing you gave it everything you had will linger long after the sting of your loss has faded. As British writer Brittany Renée put it, *"I would much rather have regrets about not doing what people said, than regretting not doing what my heart led me to and wondering what life had been like if I'd just been myself."*

The great tragedy in life is not discovering that your idea or dream was unattainable. The monumentally greater tragedy is never setting out to fully pursue it because it seemed too absurd. One of the most haunting questions that follows a person all their life is, "What if?" "What if I'd gone ahead and pursued that seemingly absurd dream or idea?" If you go for it, win or lose, you silence that question forever. And that, my friend, is a silence immeasurably worth living with.

Earlier in my life my dream was to become a top ranked tennis pro. For about three years I gave it everything I had; traveling around the world, playing tournaments week after week. In the end I simply wasn't good enough to secure the ranking I had hoped for. But the one great victory I took away from those years was this – *no regrets*. I can honestly say I laid on the line everything I had to work with. And it has saved from looking back on my tennis dream and asking the question, "What if?"

A willingness to set aside practicality for the time being – As I mentioned in the last chapter, one of the things that most quickly aborts the possibility of a new advance is the issue of practicality. Far too many radically innovative ideas have died in the womb of creativity because they were cut off at inception by a premature concern for feasibility.

One of the most important ingredients for discovering new avenues of thought is a willingness to take one's foot off the brake of practicality and press down hard on the pedal of possibility. Only in risking the danger of being too far out there will dreams and possibilities big enough to matter begin to emerge. As T.S. Eliot put it, *"Only those who will risk going too far can possibly find out how far one can go."*

This is not to say that practicality and feasibility do not matter. Of course they do. But until people are given permission to think and dream without being fettered by the chains of realism, they can never enter the stratosphere of no-holds-barred thinking. It is what I like to call "blue sky thinking"; letting one's mind soar as high as it will without worrying about the practical details. And it is in this place of daring and seeming absurdity that the dreams which ultimately make the most practical difference are birthed. A great example of this is described in *Bits and Pieces*:

Some years ago an energetic young man began as a clerk in a hardware store. Like many old-time hardware stores, the inventory included thousands of dollars' worth of items that were obsolete or seldom called for by customers. The young man was smart enough to know that no thriving business could carry such an inventory and still show a healthy profit. He proposed a sale to get rid of the stuff. The owner was reluctant but finally agreed to let him set up a table in the middle of the store and try to sell off a few of the oldest items. Every product was priced at ten cents. The sale was a success and the young fellow got permission to run a second sale. It, too, went over just as well as the first. This gave the young clerk an idea. Why not open a store that would sell only nickel and dime items? He could run the store and his boss could supply the capital.

The young man's boss was not enthusiastic. "The plan will never work," he said, "because you can't find enough items to sell at a nickel and a dime." The young man was disappointed but eventually went ahead on his own and made a fortune out of the idea. His name was F.W. Woolworth.

Years later his old boss lamented, "As near as I can figure it, every word I used in turning Woolworth down has cost me about a million dollars!"

When Copernicus first began contemplating the possibility that the earth revolved around the sun rather than visa-versa, it seemed utterly absurd to those around him. But still he pressed on, blue-skying one of science's most important discoveries!

Thus far we have seen that coloring outside the lines requires significant amounts of courage.

65

Courage to re-examine old assumptions. Courage to challenge them when necessary. And finally, courage to discard them when the best evidence favors doing so.

It also requires the eagerness to explore new avenues of thought. Outside the box thinking is never done well by vanilla lovers; those easily satisfied souls who are quietly content with conventional thinking and possessing no desire to venture out into the potential storms of perspective upheaval. It is only the true vanilla busters who walk boldly toward those storms; not because they love the conflict but because they relish the opportunity to grab hold of the lightning bolts of fresh and innovative thinking.

While this kind of radical thinking takes courage and eagerness, it also absolutely requires one final component.

The perseverance to exhaust all possibilities.

This is part of the hard work that true outside the box thinking requires. Vital insights and significant discoveries of truth never come quickly, easily, or free of charge. They are brought forth through sweat, effort, and long periods of time. And very often, it is not the smartest, the cleverest, or the most imaginative that brings home the bacon at the end of the day. It is the most doggedly persevering. This is exactly what Einstein was referring to when he noted, *"It's not that I'm so smart, it's just that I stay with problems longer."*

One of the greatest examples of this is someone I alluded to earlier - Thomas Edison. He performed over 10,000 experiments before discovering the right filament for the light bulb. His assistant at one point said in exasperation, "We have tried thousands of experiments and they have all failed. We've had no results whatsoever." To which Edison replied, "Results? Why, man, I have gotten lots of results! If I find 10,000 ways something won't work, I haven't failed. I am not discouraged, because every wrong attempt discarded is often a step forward...." In persevering it helps immeasurably to have this kind of optimistic outlook on things. Edison kept persevering after each failure and finally hit the jackpot. When someone tried to pin Edison's success on his genius, the wizard of Menlo Park responded, *"Genius? Nothing! Sticking to it is the genius!... I've failed my way to success."*

The ability to persevere in exhausting all possibilities requires at least two fundamental, underlying beliefs. Without these it will be very difficult to sustain the mental endurance necessary to take one's thinking to the highest summit. And almost always it takes this kind of creative tenacity to find the blueprints for one's extraordinary dream.

The first is the realization that **great possibilities for advancement are frequently dismissed** *solely because they also have great possibilities for abuse.* Almost everything that can bring great benefit can also bring great harm. Dynamite was originally invented with the intent of helping mankind in construction, tunnel building, etc. In a very short period of time it was also being used for the destruction of mankind. Was Alfred Nobel wrong for utilizing his creative genius in developing this powerful explosive? Of course not, but his contribution did end up being abused through no fault of his own.

Or consider this letter from Gov. Van Buren to President Andrew Jackson concerning the potential dangers of a new form of transportation called "railroads":

January 31, 1829

To President Jackson,
The canal system of this country is being threatened by the spread of a new form of transportation known as "railroads." The federal government must preserve the canals for the following reasons:

One. If canal boats are supplanted by "railroads", serious unemployment will result. Captains, cooks, drivers, hostlers, repairmen and lock tenders will be left without means of livelihood, not to mention the numerous farmers now employed in growing hay for the horses.

Two. Boat builders would suffer, and towline, whip and harness makers would be left destitute.

Three. Canal boats are absolutely essential to the defense of the United States. In the event of the expected trouble with England, the Erie Canal would be the only means by which we could ever move the supplies so vital to waging modern war.

As you may well know, Mr. President, "railroad" carriages are pulled at the enormous speed of fifteen miles per hour by "engines" which, in addition to endangering life and limb of passengers, roar and snort their way through the countryside, setting fire to crops, scaring the livestock and frightening women and children. The Almighty certainly never intended that people should travel at such breakneck speed.

Martin Van Buren – Governor of New York

The reason I bring this up is that I've noticed over the years how many times a bold, imaginative idea is dismissed by others simply on the basis that it could be abused. It is what has often been referred to as "slippery slope logic"; a small-minded attempt to discount something simply because it has the potential to slide downward in a bad direction. Just listen for this in your interactions during the next week. I think you will be stunned to see how often something that is novel or a bit outside the box is rejected solely because it *might* be abused.

In my mind this is one of the weakest arguments possible for dismissing an idea, but it happens all the time. Potential abuse does not negate the power and benefit of a radically innovative paradigm.

Vaccines were initially opposed because of the supposed potential abuse that animal diseases would be spread to mankind. Jenner was sneered at and it was reported that, *"Some serious minded men said that all animal diseases would be transferred to the human race. Some said they had actually seen horns growing out of the foreheads of innocent people."* But can one imagine where we would be today without them? In fact, one could make the argument (very forcefully I believe) that one of the best criteria for considering a new idea is that *it absolutely could lead in a bad direction!* If it can't, it's probably too milk toast to be worth one's time anyway.

The second critical belief concerning this perseverance is that **exhausting creativity and mind-numbing searching will pay off.** This is no easy certainty to come by. All too often we quit paying the price that seizing the best requires because we lose heart. Lose heart that our diligence will ever win the day. Thomas Edison was exactly right, *"Many of life's failures are people who did not realize how close they were to success when they gave up."*

I believe this is so, so true. The old adage that "the darkest hour is just before dawn" holds especially true here. If you study the discoveries of so many new discoveries or innovative paradigm shifts, you will find that time and again they were almost completely abandoned just before the breakthrough came.

But what happens if it doesn't pay off? Can I guarantee you that if you hang in there long enough, the answer will come? No. I wish I could, but in good conscience I can't. Most of the time I believe it will, but no one can guarantee that success will always come. So why do I say in this last point that one must believe that "exhausting creativity and mind numbing searching *will* pay off." Because it will. It all depends on how one defines "pay off."

What is the ultimate "payoff" for one's sweat soaked diligence and relentless pursuit of something? Is it the actual grasping of the prize and relishing of the victory? Sometimes it is. But there is a far greater prize in life than this; one that will satisfy us throughout the remainder of our days on this earth. It is the incomparably sweet taste of being able to look one's self in the mirror and say in regards to this or that pursuit – "no regrets." This is the prize most worthy of possession at any cost. Perhaps we didn't find a new way, discover a better method, or invent a cheaper model. But we gave it everything we had! And few things can match the deep-seated satisfaction that an all out mental, emotional, and physical assault upon a personally significant issue brings. Let me say it again...the greatest pay off is not the exhilaration of innovative discovery but the ongoing satisfaction of having swung for the fence. And that, my friends, is immeasurably worth taking to our grave!

We have now seen the first two characteristics of a vanilla buster – the willingness to dream an extraordinary dream as well as the willingness to think outside the box. None of these will ever translate into real life, real action, or real results without the third critical trait of those daring to live life at full throttle. It is to this essential characteristic we now turn.

Chapter IV

Letting Go of the Trapeze

*"Life is either a daring adventure or nothing.
Security is mostly a superstition."*

Helen Keller

A catheter into the human heart? Absolutely
absurd. At least this was the opinion of everyone in
Werner Forssman's world in the late 1920's. While
inserting a catheter into the bladder was common
practice; no one, but no one, believed the human
heart could withstand such an invasion. No one but
Werner himself.

So one morning in 1929 Werner went into the
hospital where he worked, tied his lab assistant to a
table to prevent interference, inserted a catheter
into his arm, and ran it all the way into the right
atrium of his heart. He then walked up three stories
to have himself x-rayed. The rest, as they say, is

history. Werner Forssman had paved the way for heart catheterization.

In 1956 he was awarded the Nobel Prize for his efforts and contribution to medicine. In talking about his daring attempt in 1929, he noted, *"One cannot achieve the impossible without attempting the absurd."* And herein lies the third great characteristic of a vanilla buster – **the willingness to risk the seemingly absurd**.

One cannot become a vanilla-buster without the readiness to put his or her respectability on the line. To make a cutting edge difference in this world requires sooner or later taking the kind of risk that appears absurd in the eyes of most, if not all. What…man walk on the moon? That's ridiculous. What…light that comes from an electric current? Give me a break. Transmitting a voice over wires for hundreds of miles? Have you lost your mind? Give up that job with all its perks and security to do what you are most passionate about? People will think you're crazy. On and on it goes. But Forssman was right – truly one cannot achieve the impossible without attempting the absurd. Just no way around it.

Taking hold of one's extraordinary dream requires a willingness to lose the polish on one's reputation. The seizing of a life-giving, soul-enflaming vision belongs only to those courageous enough to release their grip on a safety-first, embarrassment-free approach to life.

When I wrote my first book – Revolution Within – I realized that I was going to be saying some important things that weren't going to be very well accepted by possibly the majority of the readers. But I really believed in them and felt they needed to be said. However the vanilla part of me kept whimpering, "This is your first book; there's no value in alienating your first-time readers...you can say these things in your second book after you've won your audience over by this first book...once you say it in print, you can never get it back." In other words, "Go ahead and write, but just be sure to keep your reputation intact." Finally I came to the decision that writing which is controlled by the need to keep one's reputation intact is not writing at all. It is simply image maintenance through carefully guarded words. And truly, there is hardly anything more vanilla than that!

It is so very similar to the plight of the trapeze artist. For this circus performer to fully take hold of the approaching trapeze bar there must be the full release of the bar they are holding onto. The present bar provides security, safety, and maintained control. The approaching bar provides the opportunity for further progress or a disastrous fall.

It would seem utterly absurd for anyone to risk their entire being by letting go of the sure bet presently in their hands. What happens if the approaching bar is not all that well secured? What if the handle is more slippery than one had anticipated? Suppose the ropes are not as sturdy or strong as one had been led to believe? There are so, so many good reasons why a trapeze artist should never let go of the bar in his or her hands. But without taking the risk to fully let go, the performer can never know the thrill, the daring, the excitement, and the satisfaction of moving forward and upward in their specialty. The breathtaking best is reserved only for those willing to relinquish, with all ten fingers, the familiar present. For vanilla lovers this seems absolutely absurd. But for vanilla busters it is inescapably necessary.

The best word to describe this willingness to let go of the trapeze is *courage*. And this, in many ways, is the heartbeat of what it takes to be a vanilla buster. In fact the word "courage" itself is derived from a Latin word which means *heart*. The Spanish word for "heart" – *corrazon* – is derived from the same root. Without heart, without courage; one's extraordinary dream and ability to think outside the box will remain but fantasy and theory. Yet through it, dreams explode into reality and seemingly absurd thinking is finally vindicated.

Anything that makes a nickel's difference in this world, anything that draws forth one's deepest colors, and anything that moves a person out of their vanilla zone requires this critical commodity of brave-hearted living. But what exactly is it and how does it differ from recklessness or foolhardiness?

I like to define courage as this: *The refusal to be controlled by internal fears or external circumstances and the resolve to seize the highest good regardless of the cost. It is taking the right risk at the right time in the right way for the right reason.* Courage always involves two things: letting go and taking hold; just like the trapeze artist previously mentioned. Or to put it another way, it always contains a dark side and a bright side. The dark side is the letting go, which often is nothing short of terrifying. The bright side is taking hold; which can often prove exhilarating – though not necessarily always. But if not exhilarating, at least deeply satisfying.

Letting Go

The first characteristic of courage is the resolute commitment to not be controlled by internal fears. Notice that I am very careful to use the word "controlled." Courage does not mean that our fears don't *affect* us, but rather that they don't *master* us. All of us will battle fear till the day we die. It is a permanent reality of our human condition. Therefore courage is never the elimination of fear but the overcoming of it. Fact is; there can be no courage where there is no fear. Listen to what the following vanilla busters have said about fear and courage:

"I learned that courage was not the absence of fear, but the triumph over it. The brave man is not he who does not feel afraid, but he who conquers that fear." Nelson Mandela

"Courage is resistance to fear, mastery of fear – not absence of fear." Mark Twain

"Courage is doing what you're afraid to do. There can be no courage unless you're scared." Eddie Rickenbacker, decorated WWI flying ace.

"Courage is being scared to death but saddling up anyway." John Wayne

True courage always involves fear of some kind. The great issue is not whether we are afraid, but whether or not we will saddle up anyway. People's fears come in all different forms and varieties. The list of phobias is virtually endless. Consider some of the following:

Peladophobia: fear of baldness and bald people.
Aerophobia: fear of drafts.
Porphyrophobia: fear of the color purple.
Chaetophobia: fear of hairy people.
Levophobia: fear of objects on the left side of the body.
Dextrophobia: fear of objects on the right side of the body.
Auroraphobia: fear of the northern lights.

Calyprophobia: fear of obscure meanings.

The list is virtually endless. In all this one thing remains constant - we are all fear-afflicted people. We are all uniquely neurotic. Every one of us. According to Moses, among the very first words man ever uttered were, *"...I was afraid..."* Fear is part and parcel of every person's makeup since the dawn of time. And because of this, one of the greatest dangers facing all of us is that of spending our few days on this planet as human puppets, unwittingly but powerfully controlled by the strings of our own, unique phobias. And as long as our fears are what jerk us back and forth across the stage of life, we will never be free to offer to this world what is most deeply and passionately alive within us.

There are three things we can do with our fears. The first is to **pretend.** Pretend like the fears aren't there...pretend that we aren't really that scared... pretend that we aren't absolutely petrified... pretend that we are far more competent than our interior world says we are...etc. This is the worst possible approach to dealing with our fears, for it never even allows us to get to first base in overcoming them. Until we can honestly admit what is true within, we will never be able to begin moving past what is holding us back. And the more ruthlessly honest we can be about our fears, the better position we will be in to deal with them.

One of my great fears is heights. So much so that when I have to drive over a high overpass, my palms begin sweating and I start slowing down. Trust me; you don't want to be in the car when this happens to me! One of the things that has helped me make it over the overpasses as well as other heights is simply to admit to myself that I am genuinely, unquestionably afraid. Often times "terrified" is a better word. But once I can face that fear head on, call it by name, not pretend things aren't as scary as they really are; I begin to find moving forward not quite as difficult. Still not easy, but clearly not as paralyzing.

The second thing we can do with our fears is *surrender*. Just give in. Allow them to determine the marching orders of our lives. Usually it doesn't feel like we have actively surrendered to them. But when we choose a course of action primarily because it will not awaken anxieties on the inside or arouse resistance on the outside; we have almost certainly raised the white flag of fear surrender. And we have become "puppetized"; our actions now being controlled by the strings of our individual phobias.

The third response to fear is to *overcome*. Not pretend that they aren't real and present, not surrender to their demands; but to look them square in the eye and then move right past them. This is the essence of courage, the heartbeat of genuine bravery. 0

There is a tremendous illustration of this in the movie "A Beautiful Mind", the true story of Dr. John Nash of Princeton University. Dr. Nash suffered from severe schizophrenia most of his life and was particularly influenced by three imaginary characters – a government agent, his college roommate, and a little girl. Though each of these individuals never existed; they were very, very real to the inner world of John Nash and had tremendous influence on his actions.

There comes a point in the movie where he decisively says good-bye to each of these personages. He lets them know that he will never speak with them again nor acknowledge them as real. The interesting thing is that he never stops seeing them on occasion. There is never a time when they disappear and vanish forever. But when they do appear, he refuses to engage in conversation and walks right past them. It is a tremendous portrait of courage. Not pretending, not surrendering, but overcoming – walking past one's very real fears to a very real new life of dream fulfillment.

True courage does not come easily to anyone. I realize that some people seem to be born risk-takers but I question whether that necessarily means they are courageous. It may well be that they are just adrenaline junkies, addicted to the rush of living on the edge. Again, true courage is taking the right risk at the right time in the right way for the right purpose. There is no valor in risk-taking simply for the sake of risk-taking. It is only risk-taking for the sake of a noble cause or a greater contribution that is worthy of the name courage.

What are the fears that most potently keep people chained to a vanilla life? What are the strings which most often hold us as puppets in the land of the living? While there are many, I find three central ones that keep re-emerging in mine and others' lives.

Fear of losing control: One of the great lures of vanilla living is that it is fairly easy to sustain mastery over. We all like the feeling that the thermostat of life is basically under our control. When things get a little too hot or a little too cold we love to know that with some maneuvering on our part we are pretty well guaranteed to be able to get things back into our comfort zone. What scares us to death is considering the possibility of living life to such an extreme that we risk losing control of the thermostat.

As long as I don't take too great a risk, then I don't have to worry about too great a loss. If I am careful to stay within the bounds of conventional thinking then I won't have to worry about being challenged or ridiculed. As long as I keep that deep part of me hidden I will never have to fear it being mishandled by another. On and on it goes. But the grave danger of a life that is dedicated to maintaining tight control is that it ultimately goes limp in our hands, having died internally from our own unwitting, self-induced asphyxiation. C.S. Lewis put it so well concerning the risk of life and love: *"To love at all is to be vulnerable. Love anything, and your heart will certainly be wrung and possibly broken. If you want to make sure of keeping it intact, you must give your heart to no one, not even to an animal. Wrap it carefully round with hobbies and little luxuries; avoid all entanglements; lock it up safe in the casket or coffin of your selfishness. But in that casket- safe, dark, motionless, airless--it will change. It will not be broken; it will become unbreakable, impenetrable, irredeemable."*

Fear of putting everything on the line for an uncertain outcome: If only the outcome was absolutely guaranteed, we would far more quickly sign up to become vanilla busters. If we knew that the investment would yield 15% profit with no chance of going belly up...if we knew that our spouse would really listen to our heart on the matter instead of defending themselves...if we knew that working out this hard would win more matches...if we knew that this new job would unquestionably surpass the benefits of our present one...on and on it goes. Before we lay everything on the line, before we take that huge risk, before we burn our bridges; we want to know, but know, that we have made the best choice.

Unfortunately, in matters that mean the most, we usually can't know with absolute certainty. It is possible that making that change in your portfolio will yield 15% and beyond. It is also possible that you will never see those thousands of dollars again. It could well be that your spouse will genuinely listen to your heart on what is troubling you. And it is equally possible that they will immediately begin defending themselves, point out where you were wrong, and leave you wounded on the inside. All the extra sweat and hard work may lead to a big win; but you also might have a terrible loss in spite of being better prepared than you have ever been. The new job may well be the best decision you ever made, or the worst.

Englishman Robert Scott and his party boldly set out in 1910 to become the first humans to reach the South Pole. Due mainly to unexpectedly bad weather they never made it back alive, having frozen to death eleven miles short of the supply camp. In his diary we find these words, penned shortly before the end, "...*but for my own sake I do not regret this journey, which has shown that Englishmen can endure hardships, help one another, and meet death with as great a fortitude as ever in the past. We took risks, we knew we took them; things have come out against us, and therefore we have no cause for complaint, but bow to the will of providence, determined still to do our best to the last...Had we lived, I should have had a tale to tell of the hardihood, endurance, and courage of my companions which would have stirred the heart of every Englishman. These rough notes and our dead bodies must tell the tale..."*

I'm particularly struck by his statement, "...*We took risks, we knew we took them; things have come out against us, and therefore we have no cause for complaint...*" The guarantees in this life are desperately few and far between. And if we are unwilling to lay our absolute all on the line because of the fear that it might not be appropriately rewarded, then fear's mastery over us will insure that our lives are spent never knowing what might have been.

Fear of the discomfort of radical risk taking - Moving out of one's comfort zone is always a traumatic experience at some level. To *"live in the gray twilight that knows neither victory nor defeat"*, as Roosevelt put it, has its perks. It is far more comfortable, stable, predictable, and wholly unthreatening to remain in the lowlands of vanilla living. And for that reason multitudes upon multitudes choose to make that their permanent base camp. But the life that is resolved to reach the summit of maximized potential will inevitably encounter a myriad of difficulties and discomforts.

The bitter winds of temporary failure will chill us to the bone. The snows of cynicism and the sting of personal rejection will tempt us to turn back. Henry Jowett, the English curate, put it so, so well:

"It is possible to evade a multitude of sorrows through the cultivation of an insignificant life. Indeed, if a man's ambition is to avoid the troubles of life, the recipe is simple: shed your ambitions in every direction, cut the wings of every soaring purpose, and seek a life with the fewest contacts and relations. If you want to get through the world with the smallest trouble, you must reduce yourself to the smallest compass. Tiny souls can dodge through life; bigger souls are blocked on every side. As soon as a man begins to enlarge his life, his resistances are multiplied."

Jowett is exactly right. One can evade a multitude of discomforts and sorrows by the careful cultivation of an insignificant life. But if one is daring enough to pursue a life that counts, they will inevitably discover that it is also a life that costs. There is no getting around it. And those radical enough to become vanilla busters in their generation are willing to pay a price that the timid, safety-enamored can't fathom.

Letting go not only involves a refusal to be controlled by internal fears but also external circumstances. There are always good, practical reasons why the extraordinary should never be accomplished. But the presence of difficult circumstances on the outside is never enough to send a true vanilla buster packing. He or she has something on the inside that refuses to bow to the sway of external pressures.

Columnist Michael Guido notes this, *"A sound body, a brilliant mind, a cultural background, a huge amount of money, a wonderful education -- none of these guarantee success. Booker T. Washington was born in slavery. Thomas Edison was deaf. Abraham Lincoln was born of illiterate parents. Lord Byron had a club foot. Robert Louis Stevenson had tuberculosis. Alexander Pope was a hunchback. Admiral Nelson had only one eye. Julius Caesar was an epileptic. But these men made history in spite of their handicaps. And there was Louis Pasteur, so near-sighted that he had a difficult time finding his way in his laboratory without glasses. There was Helen Keller, who could not hear or see, but who graduated with honors from a famous college."*

In 1962, Victor and Mildred Goertzel published a fascinating study of 413 famous and exceptionally gifted people called "Cradles of Eminence." They had spent years researching these outstanding lives to find the most common reasons for success. Their conclusion? The single most common denominator in each of these lives was that virtually all of them, 392, had to overcome very difficult obstacles in order to become who they were.

Rarely, if ever, is an extraordinary dream captured without there being a myriad of external conditions seeking to prevent it. *"Whatever you do, you need courage. Whatever course you decide upon, there is always someone to tell you that you are wrong. There are always difficulties arising that tempt you to believe your critics are right. To map out a course of action and follow it to an end requires some of the same courage that a soldier needs."* wrote Ralph Waldo Emerson.

As we saw at the beginning of this chapter, Werner Forssman was surrounded by a host of obstacles which could easily have dissuaded him from pursuing his extraordinary dream of heart catheterization. Virtually the entire medical world, including his superiors, scoffed at the possibility. But he made the choice - frightening as it was - that he would not be ruled by outside circumstances but by inward conviction. His courage won the day, not only for himself but also for all humanity.

The first half of courage is the willingness to let go. It is the refusal to allow inward fears and anxieties to have the final say as to how or whether we move forward. Again, it isn't the elimination of fear's presence but the overcoming of fear's paralysis; it is not escaping its touch but its grasp. The operative word here is "decide." "Decide" comes from the Latin word *decidere*, which means to "cut off." Letting go means to conclusively decide, to "cut off" all avenues of retreat or escape. As Andre Gide put it, *"Man cannot discover new oceans unless he has the courage to lose sight of the shore."*

Equally, courage is the resolve to not be governed by external circumstances, regardless of how overwhelming they may seem to be. The key operative word here is "seem." Just because a situation or circumstance *seems* overwhelming doesn't mean that it is *actually* overwhelming. There is a very big difference between what is improbable versus what is impossible, and the lion hearted remain very skeptical about something being actually impossible until all possibilities for improbable are exhausted. They relish the opportunity to prove their critics wrong and delight in accomplishing what others deemed wholly beyond their reach. As Walt Disney put it, *"It's kind of fun to do the impossible."*

The other half of genuine courage is taking hold. Simply because one lets go doesn't necessarily guarantee that one will truly take hold. Touching is not the same as grasping; and true courage requires a resolute taking hold of, not merely a casual brushing up against. What then is the practical difference between the two? This is what we will now look at.

There are five things necessary for a person's hand to courageously and tenaciously take hold of the possibility before them. They are *vision, risk, sacrifice, wisdom,* and *resolve.* I call them "the five fingers of courage."

Vision – There is virtually no way to overstate how important this facet is. In the hand imagery I would liken this to the thumb – it undergirds and supports the work of the other four. What I mean by vision is the ability to see and believe that what we are seeking to take hold of is of more value and personal benefit than what we are letting go of. It is what has often been referred to as *"envisioning a preferable future."* Unless a person is internally convinced that what they are reaching for is preferable to what they have been holding onto, there is no way they are going to risk grasping the new. Especially if it is anything remotely important.

Vision lays the foundation for courage. What I mean by this is that courageous actions are normally preceded by a renovated perspective. The word "renovate" comes from the Latin word *renovare* which means "to make new again." Only when a person is able to see the situation or opportunity in a new light, only when they are able to view it from a new perspective, only when they are captivated by a vision of what could be; will they take the risks necessary to seize the prize.

Take for instance, the crucial area of sacrifice, or giving up something important to you. As long as we focus *only* on the sacrifice; the sting of loss often becomes too hard to endure. But when one can develop a perspective of "exchange", it makes all the difference in the world. Let me explain.

If you are starving to death and I offer you a Twinkie bar, what will your response be? To take it of course. And if I then ask you to give up your Twinkie, will you do it? Almost certainly you will continue to hold tightly to the only food you have, nutritionally bankrupt as it is.

The only way I am going to get the Twinkie out of your grasp is to offer you something better in its place; sandwich, pasta, etc. In this scenario you have not really *given up* your Twinkie, just *exchanged* it for something far better. This is where vision becomes so absolutely critical. Courage is far more easily mustered and sustained when one is able to view necessary sacrifices not so much as what must be given up, but as what must be released in order to grab hold of the better. The Twinkies of vanilla living will never be relinquished until we believe that we are exchanging them for a greater and ultimately more satisfying good. And that's what the perspective of vanilla busting is all about.

Vision not only lays the foundation for courage, she nourishes it along the way. Courage cannot survive, much less thrive; without being given significant doses of perspective renewal throughout the journey. As we read earlier from President Woodrow Wilson, *"We grow great by dreams. All big men are dreamers...Some of us let these great dreams die, but others nourish and protect them; nurse them through bad days till they bring them to the sunshine and light..."* Dreams require *nursing* to bring them to fruition, and this nursing is done primarily through perspective renewal.

One of the great truths which runs throughout the course of our lives is this - *where we focus our eyes profoundly determines the way in which we live of our lives.* Or, to put it another way, our *perspective* is the gate keeper of our *practice.* If our eyes are fixed on why something can't be done, if our sights are riveted upon the seemingly insurmountable obstacles before us; there is little hope that we will muster enough courage to enter the arena of extraordinary dream chasing.

But when we are captivated by the potential of what could be, when our sights are set upon the possibilities rather than the problems; this mental lingering renews vision and rekindles passion for significant risk taking.

Risk – The second finger is that of risk-taking. As mentioned before, this is at the very heart of courage. Just as true courage always involves fear; it also inevitably includes risk. To reach out and take hold of one's extraordinary dream, to seize irretrievable opportunities, to grasp life's best; these things belong only to those willing to hazard their present security and comfort. And there's nothing easy about it. That's why it's called *taking* a risk, not *receiving* a sure thing.

Vanilla busting inevitably stations one at varying outposts of crisis. Crisis in relationship... crisis in finance...crisis in reputation...crisis in self-confidence...etc. When one focuses primarily on the risk, the crisis, and the cost; it becomes easy to lose heart and return to the land of safekeeping. But when one can gaze past the danger zone to the opportunity waiting to be seized, this renewed perspective often provides the internal firepower that helps thrust us forward.

In fact, the Chinese have a fascinating way of illustrating this. Their word for "crisis" is composed of two pictures. The first picture is that of *danger*. Guess what the second one is? *Opportunity*! Every crisis is the combination of inherent danger and awaiting opportunity. The opportunity can never be grasped without risk taking and some level of danger.

But the alternative is to keep playing safe, to never venture out of one's comfort zone, to avoid all the discomforts of significant risk-taking. But in doing so, one forfeits their sole opportunity for the kind of radical, go for broke, abandoned living we were made for.

Gary Cooper was originally offered the leading part in "Gone With the Wind." Believing it to be too risky for his career, he turned it down. The part was then offered to Clark Gable, who went on to play the part spectacularly. When Cooper heard that Gable had accepted the role, he responded, *"I'm just glad it will be Clark Gable falling on his face and not Gary Cooper."* Sometimes playing safe is the most dangerous thing we can do.

Risk taking is unquestionably costly. Very often there is an inordinately high price tag attached to it. And sometimes, it leads to tragedy.

But in the end it is less costly and less tragic than the alternative – a life squandered on the vanilla beaches of comfortable, but wholly inconsequenttial living. Or, as Oswald Sanders phrased it, to spend our lives in a *"fur-lined rut."*

Sacrifice – The third finger of courage is sacrifice. This finger is usually bruised, bleeding, and sometimes broken. It is the finger which picks up the tab for the commitments vision and risk make. As Theodore Roosevelt put it, *"It is only through labor and painful effort, by grim energy and resolute courage, that we move on to better things."*

Simply put, there is no such thing as costless courage. To launch out in pursuit of one's extraordinary dream, to exchange the safe harbor of vanilla living for the threatening seas of radical living; this always incurs multi-faceted sacrifices along the journey. Kenneth Dodge writes concerning the American Revolution -

"Fifty-six men signed the Declaration of Independence. Their conviction resulted in untold sufferings for themselves and their families. Of the 56 men, five were captured by the British and tortured before they died. Twelve had their homes ransacked and burned. Two lost their sons in the Revolutionary Army. Another had two sons captured. Nine of the fifty-six fought and died from wounds or hardships of the war. Carter Braxton of

Virginia, a wealthy planter and trader, saw his ships sunk by the British navy. He sold his home and properties to pay his debts and died in poverty."

The sacrifices required to take hold of one's extraordinary dream will come in many different shapes and sizes. Some of these costs may include:

Sleep costs - Milton rose at 4:00 am every day in order to have enough hours for his *Paradise Lost*.

Time costs - Noah Webster labored 36 years writing his dictionary, crossing the Atlantic twice to gather material. Gibbon spent 26 years on his *Decline and Fall of the Roman Empire*. William Wilberforce fought for 55 years to abolish slavery in England and the British Empire. It came as he lay on his deathbed.

Energy costs – Plato wrote the first sentence of his famous Republic nine different ways before he was satisfied. Cicero practiced speaking before friends every day for thirty years to perfect his elocution. Clyde Tombaugh was the American Astronomer who discovered the planet Pluto. After astronomers calculated a probable orbit for this "suspected" heavenly body, Tombaugh took up the search in March 1929. *Time* magazine recorded the investigation: *"He examined scores of telescopic photographs each showing tens of thousands of star images in pairs under the dual microscope. It often took three days to scan a single pair. It was exhausting, eye-cracking work--in his own words, 'brutal, tediousness.' And it went on for months. Star by star, he examined 20 million images. Then on February 18, 1930, as he was blinking at a pair of photographs in the constellation Gemini, 'I suddenly came upon the image of Pluto!"* It was the most dramatic astronomic discovery in nearly 100 years.

Sacrifice, in its many different forms, is the mortar of success; cementing extraordinary results to extraordinary dreams.

Wisdom – The fourth finger on the hand of courage is wisdom. Not every risk is worth taking, not every opportunity is worth throwing caution to the wind for. This is where wisdom comes in. Wisdom is what enables us to know which risks and which opportunities are worthy candidates.

There is a difference between courage, recklessness, and foolhardiness. A crucial difference. Custer's Last Stand on June 25, 1876 is an outstanding example of this. He had been ordered to await troop reinforcements, but chose to attack anyway. He knew, but knew, that he and his men were overwhelmingly outnumbered. He and his 200 soldiers perished within in a two hour battle; not because of his courage but his unchecked ego. What he displayed on that battlefield was recklessness, foolhardiness, and hubris. But certainly not courage. It behooves all of us to keep a close watch over ourselves to be sure that the risk we are taking is a cause genuinely worthy of the risk. I say it again; courage is taking the right risk at the right time in the right way for the right reason!

Resolve – Here is the final finger on the hand of courage. Resolve is the determined act of the will to mightily take hold of the oncoming bar. It is the resolute decision to no longer debate within one's self; to actually stretch forth one's hand, and to actually put it unreservedly on the plough. Or, to use another image, it is the unswerving commitment to burn one's ships.

This is exactly what Cortez did in 1519 after he landed on the coast of Mexico. Knowing that his men would be sorely tempted to return to the old world prematurely, he gave orders that all the ships be burned. Setting aside for the moment the fact that greed and ego appear to be the controlling motivations behind his decision, it was a brilliant move psychologically. When all hope of retreating back to safety is gone, moving forward through the dangers is the only remaining option.

Resolve is the super glue which keeps the hand of courage from slipping off the handle bar of opportunity. Without it our best intentions remain but intentions, our loftiest dreams remain out of reach, our highest aspirations go unrealized, and our potential successes are relegated to "what might have been" status. But through it, we are enabled to decisively say "no" to vanilla and "yes" to our extraordinary dream.

It requires all five fingers for the hand of courage to not slip off the bar of opportunity. Without *vision*, courage will soon lose steam and ultimately die out. Without *risk*, courage will have no punch. It will leave no significant impact or make any radical change. Without *sacrifice*, courage will have no buying power or enough currency to produce a difference. Its good intentions will remain but that. Without *wisdom*, courage will have no solid directionality. Brave hearted living will be stranded without a map or compass. Without *resolve*, courage will have no decisiveness of action. It will continue to waver between two opposing choices.

But when courage is "five fingered"; it is invigorated by vision, marked by risk-taking, funded by sacrifice, directed by wisdom, and sustained by resolve.

We have seen then, that courage always involves two things. First there is the **letting go** – relinquishing the familiar and often comfortable present. Secondly, there is the **taking hold** – boldly grasping with all five fingers the opportuneity for a "preferable future." It is refusing to be controlled by internal fears or external circumstances and seizing the highest good regardless of the cost.

But how does one practically muster the inner goods to do this? While there is no easy answer or slick formulas; I have found four very helpful principles for gaining the fortitude to seize hold of the highest good and preferable future.

1. **Identify your fear(s).** This is crucial. This is not the time to play Superman, or go Stoic. Don't try to pretend that your fears are not there or that they are less than reality. The presence of fear doesn't mean that we are wimps; it only means that we are human. Just as an alcoholic can't be helped until he/she is able to admit that they are an alcoholic, neither can fear be overcome until it is first fully faced and acknowledged. When I give a speech I am always at least somewhat fearful. I cannot begin moving past the fear until I recognize its presence and call it by name.

2. **Identify your opportunity.** Perspective is critical to overcoming fear's paralysis. In every situation we *choose* which angle we will look at it from. Kahlil Gibran is exactly right, *"Your living is determined not so much by what life brings to you as by the attitude you bring to life; not so much by what happens to you as by the way your mind looks at what happens."* We can decide to only see the difficulties, which often are

very plentiful. Or, equally, we can choose to focus on the opportunity which the difficulties surround. Alexander Graham Bell put it well, *"When one door closes another door opens; but we often look so long and so regretfully upon the closed door, that we do not see the ones which open for us."*

3. **Look fear square in the eye, but become *enamored* with the opportunity.** While we need to be aware of both the fear and opportunity, we need most of all to become preoccupied with the opportunity. In other words, to "fall in love with it"; as the word *enamor* means. The trapeze artist is aware of the bar he/she is holding to, but their eyes are riveted upon the oncoming bar. Focusing on what one is giving up tends to freeze the grip; mentally lingering on the approaching opportunity frees it. As one veteran trapeze artist put it, *"Throw your heart over the bar, and your body will follow."*

4. **Concentrate on taking the first step; it's normally the hardest.** In most cases, fear is diminished and courage is increased by the first step, faltering as it often is. As Martin Luther King put it, *"Take the first step...you don't have to see the whole staircase, just take the first step."* Looking too far down

the road of the future can paralyze us just as easily as looking over our shoulders towards the past. Just take the first step forward!

Finding the courage to risk daringly and strategically is one of the central hallmarks of vanilla busters throughout history and in our day. Winston Churchill put it well, *"Success is never final. Failure is never fatal. It is courage that counts."* From George Washington to Abraham Lincoln to Teddy Roosevelt to John F. Kennedy; all great presidencies have been marked by the willingness to risk the seemingly absurd. From Copernicus to Newton to Edison to Einstein; all great advances in science have required the willingness to risk the seemingly absurd. From Michelangelo to Da Vinci to Van Gough to Picasso, all fresh and significant advances in art have involved the willingness to risk the seemingly absurd. From Wilberforce to Gandhi to Martin Luther King to Mandela, all great civil rights movements have been spawned by a willingness to risk the seemingly absurd. On and on it goes. Werner Forssman was more right than he probably had any idea – *"One cannot achieve the impossible without attempting the absurd."* Yet it requires two more characteristics before the courage to attempt the absurd is rewarded with the achieving of the impossible. It is the first one we want to look at next.

Chapter V

The Overalls of Success

"Opportunity is missed by most people because it is dressed in overalls and looks like work."
Thomas Edison

He didn't begin to talk until he was four. At age seven his teacher considered him "addled" (confused) and unteachable. His own father concurred with the teacher, *"My father thought I was stupid and I almost decided I must be a dunce."* His mother then began to educate him herself. By age twelve his hearing had significantly deteriorated and continued to worsen until he became 100% deaf in his left ear and 80% in his right. But he had an insatiable hunger to learn and a remarkable ability to work. These two things, more than anything else, are responsible for the amazing life of Thomas Alva Edison – commonly referred to as "the Wizard of Menlo Park."

His inventions literally revolutionized modern society as we know it. He was responsible for the phonograph, the stock ticker, the movie camera, for making the light bulb commercially feasible, and hundreds upon hundreds of other inventions. He holds the record for inventions with 1,093 U.S. patents and contributed to thousands of other discoveries. So influential was Edison that *Life* magazine, in a special issue, placed him first in the list of the "100 Most Important People in the Last 1000 Years."

What was the secret to his success? While many things contributed; there was one overriding, inescapable constant – his remarkable work ethic. Listen to his own words:

"Genius? Nothing! Sticking to it is the genius!... I've failed my way to success."

"Personally, I enjoy working about 18 hours a day. Besides the short catnaps I take each day, I average about four to five hours of sleep per night."

"Genius is one per cent inspiration and ninety-nine per cent perspiration. Accordingly, a 'genius' is often merely a talented person who has done all of his or her homework."

"I never did anything worth doing entirely by accident.... Almost none of my inventions were derived in that manner. They were achieved by having trained myself to be analytical and to endure and tolerate hard work."

"Opportunity is missed by most people because it is dressed in overalls and looks like work."

Thomas Edison is a tremendous illustration of the fourth characteristic of a true vanilla buster – **the willingness to work with extraordinary diligence.** No extraordinary dream is fulfilled apart from extraordinary diligence. Let me say it again. No extraordinary dream is fulfilled apart from extraordinary diligence. Period.

There is a critical balance here. One must begin with a dream. If we have diligence without dreaming it leads to *unimpassioned duty.* A life of hard work that pays the bills but never enflames the heart.

But while one begins with a dream; one cannot, must not, end with a dream. For if we have dreaming without diligence it leads to *unrealized potential.* A life of dreaming, imagining, coloring outside the lines; but never applying enough elbow grease to see envisioned possibilities become accomplished realities.

Thoreau was absolutely right - *"If you have built castles in the air, your work need not be lost; that is where they should be. Now put the foundations under them.*" "Castles in the air", as he calls them, are our extraordinary dreams. These extraordinary dreams are the crucial starting point, for without them we will leave nothing extraordinary on the ground. But notice carefully his statement concerning work - "*Now put the foundations under them.*" The foundations he is referring to are the practical, tangible results built from all-out, bone wearying, relentless diligence. They are bought with the sweat equity which is required of all those having dreams worthy enough to pursue. And it is to this critical character trait of diligence that we now turn our attention.

What exactly is this thing called diligence? I like to define it thus - *The willingness and ability to bring the full exertion of one's capabilities to the task, challenge, or opportunity at hand. It is the full release of one's physical, mental, and emotional resources for the cultivating of a preferable future.* It is the high voltage of success, the lightning bolt of peak performance. Or, as Miguel De Cervantes put it, "*Diligence is the mother of good fortune.*"

Full exertion...full release. These two phrases capture the essence of what I mean by diligence. But there is a difference between the two. Full exertion has to do with the degree of *effort* spent on the task at hand. Full release has to do with the degree of *resource* brought to the task. Exertion has to do with work and sweat; release has to do with gifts and talents. While they are two sides of the same coin, their distinctions are critical to note.

A person can feel like they are giving a pursuit everything they have while an outsider believes that clearly they are not. When this happens, it is often a case of full exertion without full release. The person doing the work really is giving it everything they have, but they are either knowingly or unknowingly (which usually is the case) keeping a portion of their ability in reserve. The coach, teacher, parent, etc. is aware of what *could* be and becomes angry or disappointed. The person doing the work is frustrated at their response because to them (the performer) it feels like they *are* doing their best. The problem here is not that of full effort but full release. As philosopher William James put it, *"Compared with what we ought to be, we are only half awake. Our fires are damped, our drafts are checked. We are making use of only a small part of our possible mental and physical resources."*

On the other hand, one can bring to the table everything they have ability-wise (full release); but their exertion can be less than full out. Often they are relying on their gifting to minimize the need for full exertion. Sadly, we see this all the time. Athletes dripping with talent but unwilling to pay the price to be their absolute best. Students with brilliant intellects choosing to get by with only partial utilization of their gifting. Gifted businessmen satisfied to employ only a small percentage of the natural talents they possess. On and on it goes. I like the way Michael Jordan put it, *"I've always believed that if you put in the work, the results will come. I don't do things half-heartedly. Because I know if I do, then I can expect half-hearted results."*

When both full exertion and full release are brought together it becomes an awesomely powerful display of unleashed humanity. This dual combination is how you account for lives like Abraham Lincoln, Thomas Edison, Albert Einstein, Michael Jordan, and many, many others. And the failure to bring both together is how one accounts for the myriad of lives that fall short of their full potential.

What causes individuals to stop short of bringing both full exertion and full release to the table of personal productivity? While there are many reasons, I believe there are three primary culprits.

Believing that easy street is the best road life has to offer.

People's behavior is always governed by their hidden, underlying beliefs. As King Solomon put it concerning man, *"As he thinks in his heart so is he."* A life characterized by minimal exertion, short cuts, and careful sweat preservation is rooted in a belief system. Central to that belief system is the underlying conviction that easy street is the best road life has to offer. And as long as one chooses to believe this; then all out, unreserved, sweat soaked diligence will be seen as a downgrade in the quality of one's life.

This is why exhortations to try harder fall on deaf ears for those in this camp. *Actions which reflect mediocrity are rooted in beliefs that revere mediocrity.* Of course the person characterized by this does not see it as mediocrity. They think of it in kinder, far more palatable terms. But at the end of the day it is mediocrity, however one wants to term it.

Until a person can see and believe the immense value of choosing diligence over half-heartedness, nothing substantial in their actions will change. They must become convinced that there is ultimately more satisfaction and reward in diligence than mediocrity.

This is why the need for visualizing a preferable future is so vitally important. Until one can see that the rewards of diligence outstrip the temporary ease of half hearted effort, they are unlikely to make much change. Extraordinary dreams are only accomplished through extraordinary diligence. But extraordinary diligence is only sustained by extraordinary vision. Vanilla busters know the fine art of continually visualizing the specifics of the preferable future they which they are working towards.

Fear that one's best will not be good enough.

Fear is the kissing cousin of laziness. Very often what appears on the surface to be lack of effort is in reality an internal defense mechanism to escape the trauma of one's best efforts just not being good enough. After all, if I don't lay it all on the line then I can always justify my defeat by whispering to myself, "They never saw my actual best. If I had given it everything I have then I would have come out on top."

But is that certain? Suppose we gave it our actual, unreserved, full out best and it wasn't good enough? Would that devastate our personal identity and sense of worth? For many it would. And one of the best ways to insure that one never feels that humiliation and pain is to keep the brakes on, at least slightly. And while it may look like a lack of effort, very often it is more about the fear of risking one's absolute best on an uncertain outcome.

I have a good friend who told me about a conversation he had with tennis great Jimmy Connors. In the course of their talking, my friend asked Connors what his favorite thing to do was. Instantly he responded, "To go out, compete, and win." Then Connors said, "And you know what my second most favorite thing to do is?" My friend shook his head and asked what it was. "To go out, compete, and lose." No doubt this helps explain why Connors was the player he was. Win or lose, he loved to lay everything he had on the line in the heat of battle. He refused to be mastered by the fear of risking one's best on an uncertain result. And nobody, but nobody can argue with the fact that Jimmy Connors left everything he had out on the court.

But how do we handle the trauma of laying out our best and then discovering that it truly was not good enough? While that discovery will typically be anywhere from disappointing to heartbreaking; there is something exceedingly crucial that our souls can take solace in – To give one's best is the best gift we can give to ourselves. Mahatma Gandhi put it so well, *"Satisfaction lies in the effort, not in the attainment, full effort is full victory."* I believe he is so very right.

My good friend Van Barry has a great perspective on all this. He notes that when it comes to doing anything worthwhile there is always pain. Either the pain of **sacrifice** or the pain of **regret**. The pain of sacrifice is the cost of doing something as well as we possibly can. The pain of regret is the cost of doing something half-heartedly and then having to live with that regrettable memory. The pain of sacrifice is temporary, but the pain of regret is much longer.

This helps immeasurably in defining what it means to "make it" in one's sport, profession, etc. Making it, in my mind has very little to do with prizes, awards, money, etc. It has everything to do with being able to look oneself in the mirror at the end of it all and say "No Regrets." Helen Hayes once said that her mother used to draw a distinction between achievement and success. She noted, *"Achievement is the knowledge that you have studied and worked hard and done the best that is in you. Success is being praised by others, and that's nice too, but not as important or satisfying. Always aim for achievement and forget about success."*

Win or lose, life's greatest reward is being able to know, but know, that we gave it everything we had. That provides a satisfaction no one else needs to reinforce.

Over-reliance upon gifts and talents

Stephen King is exactly right, *"Talent in cheaper than table salt. What separates the talented individual from the successful one is a lot of hard work."* Talent can only set the stage for success. The actual accomplishment of success requires the duet of diligence and perseverance. Sadly, many of the most talented and gifted individuals never fully play out the part they are capable of. Gary Inrig writes of this very issue from the life of Michelangelo,

Bertoldo de Giovanni is a name even the most enthusiastic lover of art is unlikely to recognize. He was the pupil of Donatello, the greatest sculptor of his time, and he was the teacher of Michelangelo, the greatest sculptor of all time. Michelangelo was only 14 years old when he came to Bertoldo, but it was already obvious that he was enormously gifted. Bertoldo was wise enough ,to realize that gifted people are often tempted to coast rather than to grow, and therefore he kept trying to pressure his young prodigy to work seriously at his art. One day he came into the studio to find Michelangelo toying with a piece of sculpture far beneath his abilities. Bertoldo grabbed a hammer, stomped across the room, and smashed the work into tiny pieces, shouting this unforgettable message, "Michelangelo, talent is cheap; dedication is costly!"

In working with athletes for thirty years now, one of the most puzzling paradoxes I have seen is this – rarely are the most gifted athletes the hardest workers, and equally rarely are the hardest workers the most gifted athletes. I have puzzled over this for years and honestly don't have any good explanation for it. It just seems to be that way and almost every coach I know observes the same thing. One thing I know for sure though – I will take effort over gifting any day of the week.

Michael Jordan was an amazingly gifted athlete. But his gifting could never have taken him to the heights he achieved were it not for his tremendous work ethic. He pushed himself relentlessly during practice and then stayed afterwards for more work on his own. At times he drove off fellow players who weren't willing to put forth the effort he thought they should. Describing his philosophy on work, he notes, *"I can accept failure, everyone fails at something. But I can't accept not trying."*

Jordan is a classic example of what happens when an extraordinary dream combines with extraordinary diligence. And the effect is multiplied even more when extraordinary talent is mixed in as well.

Having looked at three primary reasons why people fall short of full exertion and full release, let us now turn to examine more closely the work ethic of genuine vanilla busters. There are two critical components to the kind of diligence that maximizes our potential and gives us the best possible chance of seizing our extraordinary dream. It is the ability to work *hard* and to work *smart.*

Working Hard

It is one thing to work. It is a very different thing to be sweat soaked and bone weary from the day's labor. It is one thing to exercise. It is a very different thing to be gasping for air with one's leg muscles burning from all out exertion. It is one thing to study. It is a very different thing to be eye wearied and mentally exhausted from reading, memorizing, and working problems. On and on it goes. Simply because *some* effort is expended does not guarantee that *enough* effort has been spent to truly succeed. ***Working hard enough to get by, working hard enough to get ahead, and working*** *hard enough to mightily exploit one's full potential are all dramatically different things.*

I believe all of life is parabolic. What I mean by this is that the natural, physical world serves, among other things, to picture the great spiritual and personal lessons found in life. Exercise serves as a great illustration of the difference between working and working hard.

While it is true that some exercise is certainly better than no exercise, it is also equally true that not all exercise is the same. There is the light, fairly leisurely exercise of a walk around the block or even a slow jog around the track. Then there is the moderate exercise of a running a mile or two, swimming a few laps, or light weight lifting. Finally there is the all out assault on the body of sprint training, full court basketball, high intensity swimming, strenuous weight lifting, etc.

The fascinating reality about all this is that there is only one kind of exercise that significantly releases the body's beta-endorphins into our blood stream. It is the latter of the three mentioned in the previous paragraph. In order to get the natural high and energy boost which these endorphins provide, one must push the edge of the envelope.

Until we are working hard enough in our training that we are at least occasionally breathing very hard during the workout; our endorphins largely remain locked up. However, the floodgates begin to open with exertion strenuous enough that it leaves one panting. Numerous studies have shown this to be true.

Simple principle – *The kind of diligence that pushes one to the edge of exhaustion brings the kinds of rewards that lower level diligence will never know.* From my observation, most people do not exercise at a level strenuous enough for their endorphins to be significantly released. They have no idea what they are missing. Some people have medical conditions that make it unadvisable for them to exercise that hard. And they shouldn't.

But most are able to exercise at a higher level of intensity. Unfortunately, far too many will pass through this life never really knowing the natural and innate euphoria reserved only for those willing to push themselves to the edge of exhaustion.

What is true in the realm of exercise carries over to the other realms of life in general. Whether it be academics, music, drama, writing, business, medicine, coaching, etc.; the same principle holds true - *The kind of diligence that pushes one to the edge of exhaustion brings the kinds of rewards that lower level diligence will never know.* As I mentioned before, it seems to me that there are basically three levels of diligence. There is **level A** diligence – doing just enough to get by. Then there is **level B** diligence – doing enough to get ahead. Finally there is **level C** diligence - working hard enough to mightily exploit one's full potential. Only level C diligence brings home the endorphins in any arena.

When Ozzie Smith was being inducted into the Major League Baseball's Hall of Fame, one of the things he talked about in his acceptance speech was what kind of effort and performance was "good enough." He shared a slogan that he had gone back to time and again throughout his baseball career. *"Good enough is not good enough if it can be better. And better is not good enough if it can be best."* That, my friends, is level C diligence.

What then does this "level C" diligence more specifically look like, and how does one go about attaining it? Let me suggest the following:

It is a self-starting diligence. One of the clearest evidences that one is exercising third level diligence is that he or she is taking the initiative to get the process started or completed on their own. They are "ahead of the game", pressing forward to seize the best without waiting for outside pressure to be applied. They step up to the plate before their name is called; look for what needs to be done without waiting to be told, and perform to the best of their ability even when no one is looking or will ever notice. A great example of this is described in "Bits and Pieces":

He was born in Columbus, Ohio, 1890, the third of eight children. At eleven he quit school to help with the family expenses, and got his first full-time job at $3.50 per week. At fifteen he got interested

*in automobiles and went to work in a garage at
$4.50 a week. He knew he would never get
anywhere without more schooling, so he
subscribed to a correspondence home study course
on automobiles. Night after night, following long
days at the garage, he worked at the kitchen table
by the light of the kerosene lamp. His next step was
already planned in his mind--a job with Frayer-
Miller Automobile Company of Columbus.*

*One day when he felt ready, he walked into the
plant. Lee Frayer was bent over the hood of a car.
The boy waited. Finally, Frayer noticed him.
"Well," he said, "what do you want?" "I just
thought I'd tell you I'm coming to work here
tomorrow morning," the boy replied. "Oh! Who
hired you?" "Nobody yet, but I'll be on the job in
the morning. If I'm not worth anything, you can
fire me." Early the next morning the young man
returned to the garage. Frayer was not yet there.
Noticing that the floor was thick with metal
shavings and accumulated dirt and grease, the boy
got a broom and shovel and set to work cleaning
the place.*

*The rest of the boy's future was predictable. He
went on to a national reputation as a racing car
driver and automotive expert. In World War I he
was America's leading flying ace. Later he
founded Eastern Airlines. His name--Eddie
Rickenbacker.*

Vanilla busters are notorious for their self-starting diligence and initiative taking spirits.

It is a "little more" diligence. Closely aligned with self-starting discipline is the resolve to do "a little more" than is required. Whether it is non-required workouts, extra time on the piano, making additional cold calls, researching on one's own time, etc.; this habit of doing a little more than what is expected pays huge dividends over the years. Golf pro Gary Player put it well, *"The harder you work, the luckier you get."*

Fundamental to living an extraordinary life is the issue of going beyond the norm. This is inherent in the composition of the word *extraordinary* itself: *extra + ordinary*. By definition no life can be labeled extraordinary that only fills in the spaces of what is mandatory. Only when the ink of our lives begins to bleed past the lines of expected performance will the tale of our lives begin to merit the title "extraordinary." It is the "going beyond", the "little more" work ethic that is essential for this to occur. Longfellow put it so well,

> *"The heights by great men reached and kept,*
> *were not attained by sudden flight;*
> *but they, while their companions slept,*
> *were toiling upward in the night."*

In working with upcoming athletes, this is something I challenge them toward relentlessly. If they are going to exploit their potential it will require going beyond (often far beyond) what is expected. One of the most unerring indicators of a person's true commitment to becoming their best is the practicing they do when no one else is watching and when no coach is requiring it. Do they take it upon themselves to run the extra lap when everyone else is heading for the showers? Do they put in an extra rep or two in lifting weights that goes beyond what is required? Do they serve an extra basket of balls outside of practice? These are the little extras which make a big difference over time.

Larry Byrd was relentless in running extra sprints and practicing extra foul shots. Perhaps not as gifted as some of the other greats, his "little more" work ethic made up for it and earned him a place as one of basketball's greatest.

When a college coach will ask me about a player I'm working with, this "little more" work ethic is one of my very first points of reference. I will tell the coach that so and so is "a little more" athlete or they are not. In my mind this is the litmus test of whether an athlete is truly self motivated or not.

The "little more" work ethic is critical for much more than sports. It is what separates the good from the best most times. The employee who consistently gets to work a few minutes before they are required and works a few minutes later than necessary will soon catch the attention of the boss. The babysitter who always leaves the house a little cleaner than they found it will gain referrals. The executive who makes sure his presentations are reliably a little over the top of what anyone expects will find it paying off over time. Aristotle is exactly right, *"Excellence is an art won by training and habituation...We are what we repeatedly do. Excellence, then, is not an act but a habit."*

Sooner or later we all discover that our greatest obstacle in life is ourselves. It's not the people around us or the circumstances in front of us that cause us our greatest problems. It is the downward pull of our lower nature within us that most hinders our progress in life.

Equally, our greatest conquests in life are victories over ourselves. To press on when everything in us says quit, to restrain our tongues from lashing out in revenge, to refuse to pad the expense account, to choose the high road in spite of its monumental difficulty; these are the highest conquests known to man. Sir Edmund Hillary was the first man to climb Mt. Everest. In summarizing his epoch achievement he said, *"It's not the mountain we conquer but ourselves."* Exactly, but exactly.

Developing a "little more" work ethic is one of the most powerful ways to conquer ourselves and reach the summit of maximized potential. Yet this excellence of diligence must be coupled with one other feature for sweat equity to gain its highest purchasing power.

Working Smart

The story is told of an old woodsman who was working together with several younger, stronger woodsmen. One day around lunch one of the young men said, "Old man, I bet you were something in your day. Too bad you ain't got it anymore." To everyone's amazement the elder challenged the younger to a tree cutting contest the next day. The young man gladly took the challenge, believing there was no way he could lose to the old woodsman.

The next day the two of them began early in the morning chopping away furiously. The woodsmen noticed an interesting thing though about the older man. About every two hours he would take about a ten minute break. At the end of the day the elder woodsman had cut down substantially more trees than the younger. Everyone was completely amazed, not knowing how this could happen. Finally one of the men asked the old woodsman why he took so many short breaks and what he did during them. With a twinkle in his eye he replied, "The most important thing I could. Sharpening my axe." Therein lay the secret of his success. He not only worked hard, but most of all, he worked smart. He made sure he was not swinging with a blunted blade.

Beware of the danger of blunted diligence. This is energy that is expended without really making a difference. Alfred Montapert put it so well, "*Do not confuse motion and progress. A rocking horse keeps moving but does not make any progress.*" Activity and accomplishment are two very different things. Exhaustion can be the result of great productivity or well-intentioned but misdirected strivings. Hard work is essential for success in any field, but its sweat must drip along the best lines to gain maximum benefit. And often the best paths for peak performance are not the widest or most visible. This is why we all need to take time out frequently to sharpen our axe. Solomon noted this very thing, "*If the ax is dull, and one does not sharpen the edge, then he must use more strength; but wisdom brings success.*"

Again, Thomas Edison serves as a tremendous example of one who was careful to keep his axe sharp.

"*Being busy does not always mean real work. The object of all work is production or accomplishment and to either of these ends there must be forethought, system, planning, intelligence, and honest purpose, as well as perspiration. Seeming to do is not doing.*"

I love his observation, *"Seeming to do is not doing."* Busyness and productivity are two very different things. One of the grave dangers of busyness is that it often serves as "an anesthetic to deaden the pain of an empty life", as Howard Hendricks puts it. As long as we stay on the go, work long at the office, maintain a frenetic existence; we remain safe within the walls of seeming productivity. Incessant activity can serve as one's drug of choice to numb out those parts deep within that are longing desperately for more out of life.

This is why there is sometimes a hidden danger in diligence. It is all too easy to enjoy the satisfaction hard work brings and forget to be concerned as to how effective the efforts have been. "Just do it!" is a great slogan if it is being done the most effective way. However if it is not, the work not only may be ineffective but downright counterproductive.

Pat Croce, former owner of the Philadelphia 76ers has a great statement about the danger of working without proper direction. Playing off the often heard maxim, "Practice makes perfect"; he notes, *"Practice does not make perfect, it makes permanent. Only perfect practice makes perfect."* I love that statement. It is so, so true. If one is practicing in the wrong way it would be better not to practice at all. And whether it is sports or any other field, diligence only counts if the axe is being swung in the right direction. And it counts most when the blade is kept continually sharp. At all costs, sharpen the blade!

It is only through extraordinary diligence that extraordinary dreams are brought to pass. A diligence which fully releases all one's gifts, talents, and abilities. A diligence which fully exerts all one's mental, emotional, and physical strength. A diligence which is not afraid to make "a little more" the hallmark of one's work ethic. And a diligence that not only works hard but smart; taking care to keep the axe sharp. Yet there remains one final, crucial characteristic for becoming a true, all out vanilla buster...

Say "No" To Vanilla

Chapter VI

The Glory of the Grind

"Nothing in the world can take the place of persistence. Talent will not; nothing is more common than unsuccessful men with talent. Genius will not; unrewarded genius is almost a proverb. Education will not; the world is full of educated failures. Persistence and determination alone are omnipotent."

President Calvin Coolidge

Abraham Lincoln. Perhaps the greatest president in American history. And also one of the most unlikely. Born in the backwoods of Kentucky, deprived of any significant schooling; he made his mark on American history through hard work, a quick wit, keen intellect, and most of all – a dogged, never say die, determination to persevere. His entire life was a testimony to the power of relentless persistence. He suffered considerably more political defeats than victories, battled many bouts of deep depression, was ridiculed by opponents in both the North and South, and never saw the real fruit of his labor. Yet history has more than vindicated Abraham Lincoln and this nation owes an incalculable debt to this president who refused to play safe or throw in the towel. His record, however, isn't what you might expect:

- Lost job, 1832
- Defeated for legislature, 1832
- Failed in business, 1833
- Elected to legislature, 1834
- Sweetheart (Ann Rutledge) died, 1835
- Had nervous breakdown, 1836
- Defeated for Speaker, 1838
- Defeated for nomination for Congress, 1843
- Elected to Congress, 1846
- Lost re-nomination, 1848
- Rejected for Land Officer, 1849
- Defeated for Senate, 1854
- Defeated for nomination for Vice-President, 1856
- Again defeated for Senate, 1858
- Elected President, 1860

Did you catch the box score? 12-3. Twelve decisive defeats or heartbreaks against three victories. That means 80% of the major events of his life were setbacks. Think of it. If you knew that four out of five times you took the field you were going to get flattened, would you keep suiting up? Fortunately for this country, "Honest Abe" did just that.

Abraham Lincoln is an outstanding example of the fifth and final characteristic of every true vanilla buster – *the willingness to persevere against all odds*. His relentless, never say die, rugged determination to see things through to the very end is summarized in his own words, *"I am a slow walker but I never walk backward."* His law partner, William H. Herndon, wrote of him,

"Mr. Lincoln was a peculiar man; he was intensely thoughtful, persistent, fearless, and tireless in thinking. When he got after a thought, fact, principle, question, he ran it down to the fibers of the tap root, dug it out, and held it up before him for an analysis, and when he thus formed an opinion, no man could overthrow it; he was in this particular without an equal." Lincoln was not the brightest, most eloquent, or gifted politician of his day. But he overcame all odds by an exceptional work ethic and unrelenting perseverance.

What exactly then is this thing called "perseverance" and how does it differ from the characteristic we last looked at - diligence? Why is it so important and how does one go about developing it? These are the key issues we want to look at in this chapter.

I like to define perseverance as this: *It is the staying power which transforms diligence into maximum productivity. It is characterized by an abiding tenacity which overcomes all obstacles, endures all adversities, utilizes all resources, and seizes all opportunities so that one's best may be fully deposited on the playing field of life.*

It is the superglue of success, the relentlessness of high achievement. By it the tortoise beat the hare, the snail reached the ark, and the little engine that said "I think I can" climbed the hill. More importantly, by it Washington crossed the Delaware, Columbus discovered the new world, Sir Edmund Hillary climbed Mount Everest, and Michelangelo painted the Sistine Chapel. And most importantly, it is still the means by which untold multitudes of unheralded men and women in all walks of life maximize their full potential. As Napoleon put it, *"Victory belongs to the most persevering."*

If, as I suggest, it is perseverance which transforms diligence into maximum productivity; what then, is the difference between the two? While there is much overlap between them, there are some very important distinctions.

First, diligence has to do with the *amount* of effort applied to the task; perseverance has to do with the *length* of effort. It is one thing to work hard; it is a very different thing to work long.

Secondly, diligence requires the fortitude to not *give in*. To not give in to the pull in all of us to take it easy, to keep ourselves distanced from the kind of toil, pain, and weariness that all out diligence exacts.

Perseverance, on the other hand, requires the fortitude to not *give up*. To not give up paying the price diligence requires day after day, week after week, month after month, and many times...year after year. To not give up believing in a dream which seems a mockery much of the time. To not give up putting one foot in front of another when everything in you is screaming to quit. To not give up showing up again, and again, and again... When it's all said and done vanilla busting and dream chasing is much more like a marathon than a hundred yard dash. The fulfillment of one's extraordinary dream almost always requires extraordinary patience demonstrated over an extraordinary length of time.

It is very, very possible to have diligence without perseverance, or perseverance without diligence. There are those who work very hard, but have very little staying power. They are like a thunderstorm in the desert – a quick burst but soon finished. Others have great staying power but exert minimal effort along the way. They are like the heavy mist which hangs on and on, but never brings any real rain.

When one has diligence without perseverance it results in *unrealized potential*. One can bring forth tremendous effort now and then, but without this diligence being sustained over the long haul there will be large regions of potential left unmined. Mike Lupica writes the following account of how seeing unrealized potential around him spurred Deion Sanders to be sure it didn't end up within him.

Deion "Prime Time" Sanders, outfielder for the Atlanta Braves and cornerback for the Atlanta Falcons, is the only athlete to have hit a Major League home run and scored an NFL touchdown in the same week. Sanders grew up on the mean streets of Fort Myers, Fla., where exposure to some would-be athletes spurred him to make a success of himself. He explains: "I call them Idas. 'If I'da done this, I'd be making three million today...If I'da practiced a little harder, I'd be a superstar.' They were as fast as me when they were kids, but instead of working for their dreams they chose drugs and a life of street corners. When I was young, I had practice; my friends who didn't went straight to the streets and never left. That moment after school is the moment we need to grab. We don't need any more Idas."

On the other hand, perseverance without diligence brings about *perfected mediocrity*. The long haul guarantees nothing in and of itself. Mediocre efforts sustained over a long period still produce mediocre results. It is only when great perseverance is coupled with great perspiration that maximized potential begins to emerge.

The importance of perseverance can hardly be overstated. Let me provide you with several reasons why it is such a critical commodity.

Perseverance turns diligence into productivity. It is one thing to work *diligently*; it is a very different thing to work *productively*. For this to occur time is very often the determining factor.

There is a great story concerning this vital reality from an American teacher living in India. Early one morning she left the village where she dwelt to walk to another one several miles away. As she was walking along the road she came across an aged man sitting atop a boulder with a hammer in hand. He was quietly hammering upon the rock, carefully watching where his blows were landing. The lady thought to herself, "Poor man, he must be demented or spent too much time in the sun." Late that afternoon she came across the same man doing exactly what he had been doing that morning. By now there were some people around him, laughing at him.

Suddenly, the entire rock split in two after one of his well directed blows. The people were astonished, but none more than the lady. Unable to contain her curiosity she went up to the man to find out how he did it. Assuming it had to do primarily with the strategic placement of his hammer blows, she asked, "Which blow was most important? The first where you chose the spot you would work on, or the last when you finally knew the time had come for it to split?" The aged man smiled and replied, "The most important blow...was each single one." He then went on to explain that he had no way to know which blow would ultimately split the rock, only that each well directed strike played its own critical part in the outcome.

What an important lesson! The vast majority of the time we don't know which blow will split open the rock we are hammering. Einstein wrote, "*I think and think for months and years. Ninety-nine times, the conclusion is false. The hundredth time I am right.*"

As a writer I have discovered that perseverance is so, so crucial. The great issue in writing is not writing, but rewriting. That means going over what has been written time after time, after time, after time; until you feel like you've pretty much hit the bull's eye of what you want to communicate. And that is usually a lengthy and arduous process. Many times it means throwing away five hours' worth of writing and starting all over again. Also, perseverance is critical to getting published in the first place. I wrote pretty consistently for ten years before anyone was willing to publish one of my pieces. And even that was because of a chance encounter at a party which I almost decided not to attend! You just never know when the boulder is going to split. But if you don't keep hammering away, you have no chance to be around when it finally does.

The critical issue is to keep showing up, showing up, showing up. Edison had no idea which experiment would finally produce the usable light bulb, he just kept hammering away, hammering away, hammering away. Finally after literally thousands of blows, the rock split open. Charles Kettering, the famous inventor wrote, *"An inventor fails 999 times, and if he succeeds once, he's in. He treats his failures simply as practice shots."*

So many of the great successes in life are not won because of superior ability; but because of relentless showing up. Theodor Geisel, better known as Dr. Seuss, had his first book turned down by 27 publishers before one finally picked it up and launched his career. He just kept showing up. The authors of "Chicken Soup for the Soul", Jack Canfield and Mark Victor Hansen, had their first work rejected by 140 publishers before they found one who would take a chance on them. But they kept showing up, and their remarkable tenacity has been more than vindicated. As Isaac Newton put it, *"If I have made any valuable discoveries it has been owing more to patient attention than to any other talent."*

Perseverance turns adversity into opportunity. The great issue in life is not what happens to us, but how we *respond* to what happens to us. The cliffs of adversity send some men packing, while others view them as a fresh challenge to be conquered. It all depends on one's perspective.

It is much like the two cowboys in the old West who came across a poster promising ten dollars for every coyote skin brought in from the mountains surrounding a particular ranch. They set out with high hopes to strike it rich. The second night they were fast asleep around the campfire when one of them awoke to see about forty pairs of red eyes surrounding them, accompanied by the low growls of coyotes ready to attack. Immediately he turned to his buddy and said, "Quick Bubba, get up. We're rich." Now there's a great perspective on adversity!

Every adversity can be seen as an occasion for personal destruction or an opportunity for unexpected achievement. Vanilla busters are able to summon extraordinary perseverance because they see adversity not so much as an obstacle, but as an invitation. An invitation to triumph over circumstances which seem to mock success. An invitation to defy the odds and to prove the naysayers wrong. They refuse to throw in the towel because deep within their spirit is a steel resolve to not allow themselves to be conquered by the conquerable. Gene Getz describes this very thing,

In 1924, two climbers were part of an expedition that set out to conquer Mount Everest. As far as is known, they never reached the summit;

and they never returned. Somewhere on that gigantic mountain they were overpowered by the elements and died. After the failure of the expedition, the rest of the party returned home. Addressing a meeting in London, one of those who returned described the ill-fated adventure. He then turned to a huge photograph of Mount Everest, mounted on the wall behind him.

"Everest," he cried, "we tried to conquer you once, but you overpowered us. We tried to conquer you a second time, but again you were too much for us. But, Everest, I want you to know that we are going to conquer you, for you can't grow any bigger, and we can!"

Einstein was right, *"In the middle of difficulty lies opportunity."* Perseverance is the only true golden wand that can transform the difficulties of overwhelming adversity into the rewards of seized opportunity.

Perseverance prevents failure from being final. There is no way to become a vanilla buster without failing periodically, if not often. Success never, ever, ever lies in the ability to avoid failure at all costs. A fail-free life is inevitably a risk-free life; and a risk-free life is assuredly a progress-free life. As Michael Jordan put it, *"I've missed more than 9000 shots in my career. I've lost almost 300 games. 26 times, I've been trusted to take the game winning shot and missed. I've failed over and over*

*and over again in my life. And that is why I succe-
ed."*

Haddon Robinson describes the true account of
one man who learned what it is to prevent failure
from being final:

*"New Year's Day, 1929, Georgia Tech played
University of California in the Rose Bowl. In that
game a man named Roy Riegels recovered a
fumble for California. Somehow, he became
confused and started running 65 yards in the
wrong direction. One of his teammates, Benny
Lom, outdistanced him and downed him just before
he scored for the opposing team. When California
attempted to punt, Tech blocked the kick and
scored a safety which was the ultimate margin of
victory.*

*That strange play came in the first half, and
everyone who was watching the game was asking
the same question: "What will Coach Nibbs Price
do with Roy Riegels in the second half?" The men
filed off the field and went into the dressing room.
They sat down on the benches and on the floor, all
but Riegels. He put his blanket around his
shoulders, sat down in a corner, put his face in his
hands, and cried like a baby.*

*If you have played football, you know that a
coach usually has a great deal to say to his team
during half time. That day Coach Price was quiet.
No doubt he was trying to decide what to do with
Riegels. Then the timekeeper came in and*

announced that there were three minutes before playing time. Coach Price looked at the team and said simply, "Men the same team that played the first half will start the second."

The players got up and started out, all but Riegels. He did not budge. the coach looked back and called to him again; still he didn't move. Coach Price went over to where Riegels sat and said, "Roy, didn't you hear me? The same team that played the first half will start the second." Then Roy Riegels looked up and his cheeks were wet with a strong man's tears.

"Coach," he said, "I can't do it to save my life. I've ruined you, I've ruined the University of California, I've ruined myself. I couldn't face that crowd in the stadium to save my life."

Then Coach Price reached out and put his hand on Riegel's shoulder and said to him: "Roy, get up and go on back; the game is only half over." And Roy Riegels went back, and those Tech men will tell you that they have never seen a man play football as Roy Riegels played that second half."

The great question is not whether we will falter or err, but what will we do with our failures? Will we give up because of discouragement? Or will we go out and play the second half?

Perseverance enables us to stay around long enough to gain wisdom from our mistakes.

139

Charles Kettering made the insightful observation that we must learn to fail *intelligently*. He said, *"We need to teach the highly educated man that it is not a disgrace to fail and that he must analyze every failure to find its cause. He must learn how to fail intelligently, for failing is one of the greatest arts in the world."* This is so critical. There is no valor or benefit in making the same mistakes over and over and over. That is not so much perseverance as it is stupidity. The kind of relentless persistence which ultimately wins the day is not uninformed persistence. And one of the primary places our education most deeply takes root is in the classroom of failure.

Here are three suggestions someone has given for turning failure into success:

- *Honestly face defeat; never fake success.*
- *Exploit the failure; don't waste it. Learn all you can from it; every bitter experience can teach us something.*
- *Never use failure as an excuse for not trying again.*

Elsewhere Kettering wrote, *"Once you've failed, analyze the problem and find out why, because each failure is one more step leading up to the cathedral of success."* Indeed I believe he is exactly right - Learning to fail well is a **huge** component in building one's cathedral of success.

We must not only learn to fail well, but also refuse to allow failure to have the final say. Denis Waitley puts it so well, *"Failure should be our teacher, not our undertaker. Failure is delay, not defeat. It is a temporary detour, not a dead end. Failure is something we can avoid only by saying nothing, doing nothing, and being nothing."* I love his statement, *"Failure should be our teacher, not our undertaker."* The worst thing failure can do to a man or woman is to bury them in the sod of dream resignation. When we decide that we have tried for the last time because it is just too hard to try again; then, and only then, have we truly failed. Churchill put it well, *"Success is the ability to go from one failure to another with no loss of enthusiasm."*

Perseverance wears down seemingly insurmountable obstacles. This is critical for fulfilling one's extraordinary dream. President Calvin Coolidge put it so well, *"Nothing in the world can take the place of persistence. Talent will not; nothing is more common than unsuccessful men with talent. Genius will not; unrewarded genius is almost a proverb. Education will not; the world is full of educated failures. Persistence and determination alone are omnipotent."*
William Carey translated the Bible into over 40 different Indian dialects from 1793 to 1834. Though he never graduated from even high school, Carey became one of the greatest linguists the

world has ever known. This Englishman overcame tremendous obstacles and setbacks during his years in India, including the destruction of his home and much of his translation work in a great fire. Shortly before he died, he gave out his secret for success.

"If, after my removal, anyone should think it worth his while to write my life, I will give you a criterion by which you may judge its correctness. If he will give me credit for being a plodder, he will describe me justly. Anything beyond this will be too much. I can plod. I can persevere in any definite pursuit. To this I owe everything."

"I can plod...To this I owe everything." What a great description of the power of relentless perseverance. Vanilla busters owe their dream fulfillment to plodding as much as anything else. Andrew Jackson is another tremendous example of this. From "Bits and Pieces" we read this,

"The story is told that Andrew Jackson's boyhood friends just couldn't understand how he became a famous general and then the President of the United States. They knew of other men who had greater talent but who never succeeded. One of Jackson's friends said, "Why, Jim Brown, who lived right down the pike from Jackson, was not only smarter but he could throw Andy three times out of four in a wrestling match. But look where Andy is now." Another friend responded, "How did there happen to be a fourth time? Didn't they usually say three times and out?" "Sure, they were

supposed to, but not Andy. He would never admit he was beat—he would never stay 'throwed.' Jim Brown would get tired, and on the fourth try Andrew Jackson would throw him and be the winner."

Exactly! The great issue in life is not whether we get *"throwed"*, this happens to all of us. It is whether or not we *"stay throwed."*

The Greek word for "perseverance" is *hupomonee.* Literally it means to "remain under." It was used among other things to describe a plant which being crushed underfoot again and again would continue to rise back up. So is the spirit of every true vanilla buster. They overcome the crushing blows of seemingly insurmountable obstacles by rising back up again and again and again.

How then does one go about developing and sustaining this vital ability to persevere against odds? Here are some important guidelines:

Exploit the Power of Perspective. I very purposefully use the word "exploit" here. It is one thing to utilize something; it is a very different thing to exploit it. What I mean by *exploit the power of perspective* is to drain every possible ounce of benefit from it. To drink it completely dry, to seize its every advantage, to utterly maximize its possibilities. Most people are aware of the power of perspective; only vanilla busters master the fine art of exploiting that power.

Nothing is more crucial to perseverance than perspective. How we view the obstacles, challenges, and difficulties before us will profoundly determine the ways in which we respond to them. Stephen Covey is exactly right when he writes, *"Our problem is the way we see our problem."* I can say without exception that the greatest failures in my life (and there are plenty) all began with a blurred or patently wrong perspective on the matter at hand. And equally, all my greatest successes were profoundly determined by the point of view I approached them from.

One of the most important perspective realities I know of to help foster ongoing perseverance is what I like to call "the exchange principle." This is something I alluded to in Chapter 4. Simply stated, it is learning the fine art of never giving up something, but always exchanging it for something better.

Anything of significance is going to require some level of sacrifice on our part in order to attain the reward. Whether it be getting in shape, dieting, continuing one's education, competing in a sport, financial success, etc.; there is always some kind of price tag attached to it. And it is the day in, day out, payment of that price tag that can make perseverance so difficult. This is where perspective becomes so critical.

When I focus primarily upon what I must sacrifice in order to accomplish a goal; the cost can quickly feel too high. As long as I am preoccupied with the cost, I have no visionary room left to contemplate the reward. And when there is no room to mightily envision the satisfaction and reward of achieving our goals, it becomes internally disabling. It is much like what happened to Florence Chadwick, the first woman to swim the English Channel in both directions. On the Fourth of July in 1951, she stepped out into the Pacific to attempt to swim from Catalina Island to the California coast. The challenge was not only the distance, but also the bone-chilling waters of the Pacific. To complicate matters, a dense fog lay over the entire area, making it impossible for her to see land. After about 15 hours in the water, and within a half mile of her goal, Chadwick gave up. Just as she was pulled into the boat, the fog lifted and she could see the shore half a mile away. Later she told a reporter, *"Look, I'm not excusing myself. But if I could have seen land, I might have made it."*

Not long afterward she attempted the feat again. Once more a misty veil obscured the coastline. But this time she kept reminding herself of the shore that was there. Buoyed by that perspective she bravely swam on and achieved her goal. In fact, she broke the men's record by 2 hours!

When we focus only upon the cost attached to our goal, we are like Florence Chadwick swimming in the fog with no sight of the land before us. But as we take time to continually remind ourselves of the shore before us (i.e. the satisfaction and reward of accomplishment), our spirits are buoyed and we are enabled to continue persevering. Perspective determines everything!

This is why I think it is so crucial to always view sacrifice in light of reward. It is only this perspective which enables us to move from the *giving up* of something to the *exchanging* of it for something better (as I previously discussed in chapter four). In fact the very word "exchange" comes originally from the combining of two Latin words which mean *"to barter out."* It is the reward of the pursuit that has the bargaining power to outbid the cost of the pursuit. Without it, we will all too quickly cash in our chips.

Try to visualize a seesaw with only one person sitting on it. That person is obviously stationed on the ground. What will it take to get this person up in the air? Clearly it will require another person of equal or greater weight on the other end.

As long as we are focused only upon the cost of the task before us, we will be like the one person on the seesaw, weighted down by its heaviness and soon wearied by the responsibility. But if we can learn to mentally load down the other side with the various potential rewards that will be ours in spite of the cost, we will have a far, far greater chance at persevering.

One way I have found helpful is to think of two columns: **Cost** and **Compensation**. The cost is what the task or opportunity at hand is going to require of me. The compensation is the benefit(s) I will derive in achieving it. Now here's the key: *Until one can see that the compensation equals or outweighs the cost, getting off the ground will be very difficult.* Human nature is such that we must be convinced that the potential reward outweighs the present sacrifice or we are not likely to budge. It's all a matter of what we choose to focus on. This is why I call it the fine art of never giving something up but always exchanging it for something better.

Take physical fitness for example. My primary way of keeping in shape is about 25-30 minutes of interval sprinting. I wish I could say I enjoy the sensation of my leg muscles and lungs burning from the exertion. But I don't. Never have, never will. So why do it?

I have a list of about 20 rewards that come from the workout. At the top is how it makes me feel the rest of the day. 20 minutes of hell for feeling great the rest of the day. Often I will tell myself, "Do the math." 20 minutes of significant discomfort for 16 hours of feeling highly energized. Then I go through a litany of other reward reasons I have developed. It usually takes most of them to get me out there! Without them, I can't imagine how I could keep persevering in this particular form of exercising.

Weight Watchers does a great job of helping people with this very thing in losing weight. They emphasize not so much what you have to give up in dieting, but learning to mentally savor the outcome of passing up that piece of cake. As people focus primarily on what it will be like to drop that dress size, to feel better, to have people comment on the obvious weight they have lost, and other rewards; the hardship of giving up those extra fat grams is substantially lessened. Not surprisingly they lead the pack in weight loss programs. It's all about perspective! Exploiting it to its fullest is undoubtedly the foundation to perseverance over the long haul.

Take Time to Refuel the Inner Man. Just as a car cannot make a long trip without stopping for gas, perseverance cannot be sustained over the long haul without refueling. Look at the great vanilla busters throughout history and you will find that most were very careful to keep the inner fire burning. Here are some of the different kinds of kindling that help keep the inner drive ignited.

Reading – Reading is to the mind and spirit what food is to the stomach and body. Yet it all too often is neglected for easier, softer diversions. Mark Twain was right, *"The man who does not read good books is at no advantage over the man that can't read them."*

Oliver Wendell Holmes, Jr. was and still is generally regarded as one of the most outstanding justices in the history of the U.S. Supreme Court. He was known as the Great Dissenter because he disagreed with the other judges so much. Holmes sat on the Supreme Court until he was 91. Two years later, President Roosevelt visited him and found him reading Plato. "Why?" FDR asked. "To improve my mind," Holmes answered. Vanilla busters know nothing of retirement from personal intellectual growth.

I think it is particularly helpful to maintain a steady stream of biographies in one's reading. Few things reinvigorate the spirit more than reading about the triumphs, failures, risk-taking, and perseverance of other vanilla busters in history.

Exercise – Exercise is as important for the inner man as the outer. It not only helps keep the body in shape; it releases stress, helps reduce worry, makes thinking sharper, provides added energy, and a multitude of other benefits.

Relaxation - Ashleigh Brilliant is exactly right, *"Sometimes the most urgent thing you can possibly do is take a complete rest."* Perseverance that is not seasoned with enough times of genuine relaxing and personal recharging will ultimately end in burn out. Different things enable different people to best relax. Find what works best for you. Many times good old fashioned sleep is what the inner man needs most.

Fun – This vital element of life is too often overlooked in talking about perseverance. Few things bring renewed strength for the task, a fresh outlook on life, or rejuvenation of spirit like fun and laughter. Of course one should be wise in their choice of fun, but not stingy. Heartiness of laughter is not antithetical to living life as a vanilla buster; rather it is simply a part of daring to live life at full throttle.

Run with Other Likeminded Marathoners. It is virtually impossible to overstate how important this is. Emerson put it well, *"Show me with whom you are found, and I will tell you who you are."* When I give talks to incoming college freshmen I will normally ask them what they think the most important decision they will make in college is. Usually I get answers like "choosing your major", "how you spend your free time", etc. I then tell them what I believe it to be – who you choose as your closest friends. Nothing more profoundly affects a student's years in college than the peer group he or she chooses to run with. I've yet to find a teacher, administrator, or coach to disagree with that.

Colin Powell gives some great advice along these lines, *"Surround yourself with people who take their work seriously, but not themselves, those who work hard and play hard."* Vanilla busters do best by surrounding themselves with other vanilla busters. We all need the heat of others to rekindle our flickering flame for significant living. J.R. Tolkein, C.S. Lewis, George MacDonald, Owen

Barfield, and several other outstanding British writers were all members of a group named the "Inklings." These writers met once a week to critique each others' writings, chat about various topics, and simply enjoy one another's company. Each of them credits that group and their times together as a very significant contributing factor to their success.

The importance of perseverance in the life of a vanilla buster is virtually impossible to overstate. It is that attribute which colors every characteristic of vanilla busting. It requires perseverance to keep a tight hold on one's extraordinary dream. It requires perseverance to continue thinking outside the box until the right plan or strategy is devised. It requires perseverance to continue risking the seemingly absurd. It requires perseverance to dig deep and work with extraordinary diligence.

One of the greatest vanilla busters of all time was Winston Churchill. England and the world owe an incalculable debt to this man of steel fortitude, undaunted courage, and most of all relentless perseverance. Giving a talk to the students at Harrow School in 1941 his entire message centered around one thought - *"Never give in, never give in, never, never, never – in nothing great or small, large or petty – never give in except to convictions of honor and good sense."* Hard to find better advice than that!

Epilogue

"This is the true joy in life, the being used for a purpose recognized by yourself as a mighty one: the being thoroughly worn out before you are thrown on the scrap heap, and being a force of nature instead of a feverish selfish little clod of ailments and grievances complaining that the world will not devote itself to making you happy."

George Bernard Shaw

Rudy. The film has captivated audiences since its appearance in 1993; and in 2005 was voted one of the best sports movies from the last 25 years. It is the true story of Daniel "Rudy" Ruettiger, a vanilla buster *extraordinaire.*

I love this movie. Most of all I love the story it lets us in on. You see if it weren't for the movie, the vast majority of us would never know about Rudy Ruettiger or his remarkable story of following his childhood dream to play football at the University of Notre Dame. For Rudy was a very ordinary young man with very ordinary athletic and academic abilities from a very ordinary family living in a very ordinary mid-Western city. Rudy was just like most of us. And that's what I love so much about his story.

In this book we have been looking at a myriad of vanilla busters throughout history. Most of them have been easily recognizable – Edison, Lincoln, Einstein, etc. And while their lives have given us great snapshots into what vanilla busting looks like, it seems to me that there is a potential problem with focusing on these individuals. It can easily leave the impression that vanilla busters are high profile, high achievement, high IQ men and women. That they are la crème de la crème...the fastest, the strongest, the smartest, etc.

But the stark, undeniable reality is this: The vast majority of us much more resemble Rudy Ruettiger than Albert Einstein, Thomas Edison, or Abraham Lincoln. Maybe that's why I'm so drawn to his story. What Rudy's life screams to me is that vanilla busting is open to everyone. If a 5'6" kid weighing 165 pounds with Dyslexia and almost no athletic talent can graduate from Notre Dame as well as play on their football team...well maybe there's hope for all of us. And indeed there is; if like Rudy, we'll summon the courage to find and pursue our extraordinary dream.

The story of Rudy beautifully fleshes out the five central characteristics of a vanilla buster. Let's take a brief look at each:

The willingness to dream an extraordinary dream

Rudy's dream was to gain admission to Notre Dame and play on their football team. Problem was he lacked the grades, size, athletic ability, and money to go there. But he never lets the dream die. He marvelously exemplifies the words of Woodrow Wilson, "...*Some of us let these great dreams die, but others nourish and protect them; nurse them through bad days till they bring them to the sunshine and light which comes always to those who sincerely hope that their dreams will come true.*" Rudy had to nurse his dream through many bad days and innumerable setbacks, but he never let the dream die.

The willingness to color outside the lines

Rudy couldn't get into Notre Dame so he went to a small junior college to try and make the grades necessary to transfer in. He walked onto the team after winning a spot at tryouts. He slept in a room at the football stadium (in actuality it was the basketball arena) to save money. His outside the box thinking ultimately landed him a place inside the school.

The willingness to risk the seemingly absurd

Virtually everyone in Rudy's world thought it was absurd for him to even consider Notre Dame, much less play on the football team. As his father put it to him, "Ruettigers don't belong at Notre Dame." One of his high school teachers told him that essentially God hadn't made him smart enough to be able to go to a school like Notre Dame and that it would be foolish for him to even try.

The willingness to work with extraordinary diligence

What set Rudy apart on the ball field was his all out, never let up, remarkable work ethic. Though he never played in the games (except the last down of the last game), no one competed more fiercely or pushed themselves more strenuously in practice than Rudy. There is a great part in the movie where the head coach tells Rudy, "I just wish God would put your heart into some of my players' bodies." That same work ethic was brought over into the classroom as well.

The willingness to persevere against all odds

The entire movie is permeated with this character trait. Rudy perseveres against the skepticism of his family and friends that he could ever get into Notre Dame, much less play for the school. He perseveres through classes at Holy Cross (the junior college) until he finally gets admitted. It is there that he is diagnosed with Dyslexia and begins learning new ways to study. He perseveres through some of his fellow teammates' opposition to his work ethic which makes them look bad. He does quit the team once but comes back even more determined. He perseveres through the disappointment of a new coach initially denying him the opportunity to suit up for one game. Rudy's unquenchable willingness to persevere against all odds serves as the bedrock for his success. Other movies that powerfully and clearly portray these five characteristics of a vanilla buster are *Braveheart, The Rookie, Rocky, Hoosiers, October Sky, Goal, Miracle, Glory Road, Take the Lead,* and many others.

Rudy shows all of us, in no uncertain terms, that vanilla busting is never a matter of *talent* but *heart.* It's not about a high IQ, athletic ability, or a privileged status in society. It's about a go for your dream, never say die, take no prisoners, all out assault on life. Listen to the true Rudy Ruettiger's own words:

"Do what you really want to do. Don't let the words of others hold you back. Take a step towards your Dream. As you move closer to your Dream, new opportunities will open up for you that you never imagined possible. Along the way, the journey will be full of struggle, but I learned that the greater the struggle, the greater the victory! As you go for your dream, you will inspire others to live their dream."

What about you my friend? Will you follow in the vanilla busting footsteps of Rudy? Will you join the ranks of those who have risked going for their dream and persevered through hell and high water to attain it? Or will you go tamely and quietly into the night? Will you be one of the far too many who "*go to the grave with the song still in them*"? I hope not. I pray not. This world desperately needs what you have to offer.

Probably very little that you have read in this book is truly new to you. But please never forget this - *Just because something is basic, just because something is simple, just because something is familiar; does not mean that it is not exceedingly powerful.* The most simple, basic, fundamental things in life usually end up being the most powerful and important. What can be more simple or powerful than the exceedingly familiar statement, "Love your neighbor as yourself."? So easy to understand...so earthshaking in its power... and admittedly so difficult to do.

So let me leave you with a few simple but important closing thoughts.

It's never too late to pursue your extraordinary dream. Perhaps some of you have thought to yourselves while reading this book, "I wish I had read this when I was younger, before I had spent my life the way I have. But it's too late now to pursue any kind of "extraordinary dream."

I always chuckle internally when people talk about something being "too late" to do in life. We live in a universe that is who knows how many zillions of years old. We are part of a civilization that is over 8,000 years old. The vast majority of us live to be less than 90 years old. Our lives, at best, are a pinprick in time. But we talk about something being "too late." Give me a break! It is never too late *"to dare mighty things"*, *"to win glorious triumphs"*, to be *"actually in the arena."*

Age, for the most part, truly is a state of mind. General Douglas MacArthur put it so well, *"People grow old by deserting their ideals. Years may wrinkle your skin, but to give up interest wrinkles the soul. When the wires are all down and your heart is covered with the ice of cynicism, then, and then only are you grown old."*

History records that many people made some of their greatest contributions to society after the age of 65. The Earl of Hapsburg, for example, was 90 when he began preparing a 20- volume revision of English law. Goethe wrote Faust at 82. Galileo made his greatest discovery when he was 73. On and on it goes.

Few sights are more compellingly attractive and inspiring than white haired vanilla busters. To see someone still risking at the end of their days, refusing to allow their inner being to enter into retirement, relentlessly climbing to higher and higher ground...this person inspires more hope and dispenses more motivation than they have any idea.

It's never too early to pursue your extraordinary dream. Again, "early" and "late" are utterly relative terms when seen against the background of time itself. "Early in life" presupposes that one's existence on earth consists of a prolonged period of time. And that is a *huge* presupposition; for one never knows when the closing curtain on one's days will be drawn. What we have at the moment is only present time. We have no way of knowing whether this time is "early" or "late", just that it is present. And no one knows how long it will be present for. It behooves us therefore to do something extraordinary with our lives in the only time frame we know for sure we have – now. As James Russell Lowell put it,

"Life is a leaf of paper white
Whereon each one of us may write
His word or two,
And then comes night.

Greatly begin, though thou have time
But for a line,
Be that sublime,
Not failure, but low aim, is crime."

No one will ever be carded for their extraordinary dream. Extraordinary dreams do not require a certain age before they can be discovered, pursued, and even accomplished. Alexander conquered 90% of the known world by the age of 25. Einstein began working on his theory of relativity when he was 12. Solzhenitsyn was writing when he was 14. I say it again; it is never too early to pursue one's extraordinary dream!

There is more to you than you have any idea. If I could reach inside of you and switch on one very certain, particular light; do you know what it would be? Very simply this, *"You have more to offer than you have any idea."* Let me say it again, *"You have more to offer than you have any idea!!!"* Oh how I wish I could get you to believe that.

I don't know why you don't. Perhaps it was your family or friends telling you that you didn't have what it takes to do anything special with your life. Guess what? They were wrong. They will always be wrong. You have more to offer than you have any idea; than they have any idea. Time to quit believing that lie and start pursuing the extraordinary dream God made you for.

John Gardner puts it so well - *"There is something I know about you that you may not even know about yourself. You have within you more resources of energy than have ever been tapped, more talent than has ever been exploited, more strength than has ever been tested, and more to give than you have ever given."*

He's right you know. There resides within you the goods to make more out of your life than you've ever dreamed possible. There's only one thing needed for your life to be ablaze with purpose, passion, and significance. And that is for you to resolutely **Say 'No' to Vanilla** and to take the dare to live life at full throttle. I can't describe that journey any better than Robert Frost:

"Two roads diverged in a yellow wood,
And sorry I could not travel both
And be one traveler, long I stood
And looked down one as far as I could
To where it bent in the undergrowth;

Then took the other, as just as fair,
And having perhaps the better claim,
Because it was grassy and wanted wear;
Though as for that the passing there
Had worn them really about the same,

And both that morning equally lay
In leaves no step had trodden black.
Oh, I kept the first for another day!
Yet knowing how way leads on to way,
I doubted if I should ever come back.

I shall be telling this with a sigh
Somewhere ages and ages hence;
Two roads diverged in a wood, and I –
I took the road less traveled by,
And that has made all the difference."

Take the road less traveled. Be a vanilla buster! And may God bless you on the journey...

Made in the USA
Lexington, KY
10 June 2019

41739064R00098